White Beacons OF Atlantis

by Natalie Sian Glasson

Channeled from past-life self,
Nara Merlyn

Other books by Natalie Sian Glasson:

Twelve Rays of Light:
A Guide to the Rays of Light and
the Spiritual Hierarchy

White
Beacons
OF Atlantis

by Natalie Sian Glasson
Channeled from past-life self,
Nara Merlyn

3 LIGHT
Technology
PUBLISHING

For more information about special discounts for bulk purchases, please contact Light Technology Publishing Special Sales at 1-800-450-0985 or publishing@LightTechnology.net.

Cover Artwork by Natalie Sian Glasson

Also available as an ebook from your favorite ebook distributor

ISBN-13: 978-1-62233-041-6

Published and printed in the United States of America by:

PO Box 3540
Flagstaff, AZ 86003
1-800-450-0985 or 928-526-1345
www.LightTechnology.com

For my Mam and Dad
Thank you for your constant loving support.

For Nara and Benjamin
Thank you for helping me share your lifetime in this way that feels so personal to me.

**For all the physical and energetic souls present with me in Atlantis
who continue to journey with me in this lifetime**
You know who you are. Thank you.

Table of Contents

Preface

I became aware of my ability to channel light, love, and consciousness through my voice and the written word in 2002 at the age of eighteen years. Archangel Michael, acting as the overseer of my channel, was the first to bring forth his energies through my being, creating a strong connection that continues to this day. While many ascended masters and archangels shared their energy signatures with me, introducing their energy for later work, there was another energy that came strongly to me as I began to realize my channeling abilities. This was the energy of the Celestial White Beings.

Their energy was so intense that I felt sleepy and lethargic in its presence, unable to remain conscious. With time I became accustomed to their vibration, often seeing them bounce around my home as white energetic forms. They told me their visits could only be short because they had to become accustomed to slowing the speed of their light to connect with my physical reality. It also strained my energies to be in their presence.

Their first words to me were that they were my soul group, I was one with them, and I was here on Earth as a representative of their consciousness. While I was happy to connect with the Celestial White Beings and to be told of my soul group, I had strong inner feelings of betrayal, distrust, and wanting to push them away. I was always pleased to see them, yet an inner energy of sadness would arise in me.

The Celestial White Beings shared with me that my life on Earth now is a continuation of the lifetime I experienced with them in Atlantis. Many unneeded energy patterns I held on to and manifested in my current life actually extended from my Atlantean lifetime as Nara. The life purpose Nara created before her birth was left unfulfilled and had to be postponed to another lifetime because Atlantis fell.

Very soon after I began to channel, my guides and the Celestial White Beings encouraged me to channel a book, which turned out to be my memories of my time in Atlantis written in novel format. Through this process, I was able to master my channeling abilities while connecting with my lifetime in Atlantis, which was very important to the evolution and spiritual awakening of my current self and reality. Feelings of being lost, experiencing loss, and being unworthy or not good enough, along with fear and lack of faith in my own inner power, were energies I thought belonged to me; however, I now realize they stemmed from unresolved energies I was holding on to from my lifetime as Nara.

While that first writing was too lengthy to become a book, I was encouraged to write another one, *The Twelve Rays of Light: A Guide to the Spiritual Hierarchy*, which was published in 2010. Since then I have been trying to return to writing Nara's story, yet something always held me back. I realize now that Nara's story isn't just a story but a lifetime, my lifetime, that is occurring simultaneously with my current lifetime and affects the lives of many then and now. It is filled with all the natural human emotions and experiences — many of which I have had to release and heal within my being.

Before I could write Nara's story, I had to meet some of the important people from her lifetime in my current lifetime so that greater channels of remembrance and understanding could open and heal, allowing further freedom for Nara to express herself. These people seemed to simply walk into my life at the divine time, evoking reactions of tremendous knowing from within my being and theirs. I have had the wonderful experience of meeting people in this lifetime who are like those in the stories that follow, which has allowed a profound healing for Nara. Most importantly, I have been told by the Celestial White Beings (and feel it deep within me) that the physical people I connect with at my channel workshops are beloved friends who used to visit Nara's temple in Atlantis. This is because the Celestial White Beings and I created a contract to return to these people in this lifetime to continue to support their spiritual awakening. I extend my love, support, and friendship to you now, as we have been drawn together for a divine purpose and remembrance. I honor the connection we hold.

I feel many of my experiences in the past few years have allowed me to work with the Nara aspect of myself, creating freedom for both of us while allowing us to express ourselves as one with greater fullness. My greatest wish for this book is to offer Nara a voice through it so that she can share her wisdom and experiences of the fall of Atlantis, a time that still affects the energetic patterning and consciousness of humanity.

I also wish to reintroduce you to the beloved Celestial White Beings. Through my experiences, I have allowed myself to accept the Celestial White Beings more fully into my heart through greater understanding of the circumstances that took place at the fall of Atlantis. I have confirmed this through the fuller manifestation of their energy within my reality, channeling, and workshops as well as the manifestation of this book. All three aspects — Nara, the Celestial White Beings, and I — are now ready to share with you to aid your own healing of your Atlantean lifetime and your current reality.

How to Use This Book

White Beacons of Atlantis is principally a workbook designed to inspire your own process of healing, awakening, and remembering. It is a pathway to unlock memories of your lifetimes in Atlantis as well as reunite you with the treasure of inner wisdom and abilities waiting to emerge from your soul into your physical reality. This is a powerful and paramount time for healing and moving beyond old cycles to create a fresh, loving, happy, and enlightened perspective of yourself and your reality on Earth — essentially, to manifest and experience the era of love on Earth. With acceptance, permission, and an open mind and heart, this book can guide you to bring balance to your reality and aid the ascension of humanity.

In each chapter, Nara reminds you of your soul, inner wisdom, and personal memories of Atlantis while sharing her wisdom and renewing her connection with you. This might seem like a novel, but it is Nara's true account of her reality and experiences during her time in Atlantis. At the end of each chapter, you will find one or two practices that encourage you to experience Nara's account for yourself. The practices guide you to heal or reconnect with and explore your Atlantean self and lifetime. They are guided by Nara and are very important because they encourage you to explore your own Atlantean and current life stories.

Use this book intuitively. You may feel guided to read the entire book from cover to cover and only engage in the practices and experiences afterward, or you may wish to participate in the practices as you move through each chapter, taking more time to evolve and heal with Nara as you read. If you decide to engage in the practices at a later date, I encourage you to read through them as you go because you will create an intention for awakening and healing on numerous levels of your being. Your intuition is your true guiding light.

A glossary is provided to support further exploration and understanding of the words, ideas, and concepts Nara discusses. You may wish to read through the glossary first to familiarize yourself with the ideas, or you can simply refer to it when you need clarification.

When you do engage in the practices, read each one through a number of times to familiarize yourself with each intention and process. Nara shares many affirmations that can be empowered by speaking them out loud once or twice a day with focus and determination. Continually reciting the affirmations mentally while you go about your daily routine will empower and support the manifestation of the affirmations for your experience in your reality. Recording the affirmations using your own voice and replaying them during your sleep or meditation or even when your mind is focused elsewhere will reprogram your mind and energy, encouraging you to easily embody the affirmations. If at any time you feel a resistance to working the practices or feel you have already accomplished something similar in the past, I suggest that you complete the practice in question once. Resistance acts as signal that healing and focus are required, and often resistance is where we find the key to unlock our inner truth.

Nara's accounts and the spiritual awakening practices can be intense, drawing energies from within you that require healing or release, so it is important to be gentle with yourself and to always invite healing into your being and reality from your community of guides. Know that everything occurs for a reason and with a higher purpose. If you do find yourself overwhelmed by emotions, thoughts, visions, ideas, or energies from the past — whether it is pain you have caused another, suffering you have experienced, or simple feelings of emotional release — in times of uncertainty, when healing is required or when a vision or energy arises that you are unsure of, I ask you to use the practice that follows.

Love is always the answer. This is a story and journey of numerous forms of love. Enjoy your journey!

In love always,

Natalie

Balancing, Healing, and Grounding Practice: Cleansing Past Energies, Emotions, Thoughts, or Visions

Breathe deeply, increasing the depth with each breath and centering your thoughts on your breathing to take you into a space of relaxation. Say out loud,

I call on my angels and guides: my soul, Archangel Raphael and his angels of healing, and the angels of Atlantis. I now command and permit a deep and absolute healing to take place within all levels of my being, allowing me to enter a space of love, peace, and clarity. I cleanse, release, and erase all unneeded and inappropriate energies, thoughts, emotions, visions, and attachments from and to my past, dissolving their influence within my current reality and being.

I am surrounded in a cocoon of angelic love. I am protected by Archangel Michael and healed by Archangel Raphael. My energies are positively transformed by Archangel Zadkiel, and I am grounded and balanced by Archangel Sandalphon. Archangel Gabriel shares with me gentleness and compassion so that I may align with my inner love, power, and divine consciousness, accepting clarity and truth eternally.

I am healed. I am healed. I am healed, and that is it.

You may want to read the words out loud until you feel yourself accepting and bathing completely in the loving and pure angelic support you have summoned. Remember, your intentions are powerful: Focusing on a negative energy energizes and creates it in your reality, and focusing on positive affirmations, even when you feel uncertain, allows you to create experiences of love. There is only love in your being and reality unless you choose to believe otherwise. When you do believe otherwise, you are accepting illusions into your reality.

I also wish to share with you a very beautiful affirmation:

I am grounded, centered, and balanced, ready to continue my blissful reality on Earth.

Intentions

I am Nara Merlyn, only child and daughter of Parlo and Martyna. I have lived on the plane of Atlantis in the north countryside for twenty-two years. I chose my parents before my birth on the physical plane, creating a sacred contract with their souls to assist me in achieving appropriate learning and growth to support my adult life and purpose on Earth. Martyna gave birth to an extremely white-skinned, glowing baby with pastel-red hair and gray eyes. My birth took place in the main city of Atlantis within a birthing chamber of the Sacred Temple of Spiritual Evolution and Truth. Martyna was surrounded by rose quartz crystals that she had previously programmed with love from her heart.

Many priestesses attended the birth to hold the energy for Martyna and radiate waves of healing to dissolve all pain and discomfort we might have experienced as mother and daughter. The priestesses also filled the role of manifesting the divine plan and wisdom of my soul into my physical body for those precious first moments of life as I fully entered the physical realms of Earth. Before my birth, the priestesses communed with my soul, the very essence of my being, to determine my purpose of incarnation and the wisdom I wished to remember in my life on Atlantis. Their role was to energetically prepare all needed pathways for me from the moment I entered my life. My father was ever present, uniting his energy of love and peace from within his being with Martyna and me.

After my birth, I experienced a blessing ceremony in which the most evolved beings of Atlantis reconnected my energies to the universe and the Creator while fully grounding me in the sacred Goddess vibrations of Mother Earth. My parents were privileged to this treatment because they had been dedicated students within the Sacred Temple of Spiritual Evolution and Truth since their early child-hoods. The high priests and priestesses of the temples told Martyna and Parlo that they were to bring forward a child with whom they would share their spiritual wisdom and to move from central Atlantis to the north countryside. They were to move into greater isolation and peace to focus their attention and love on their child — me — while advancing their own alignments with the universe and the Creator. They would continue their instruction at the temples in central Atlantis through energetic and mind connection with the spiritual mentors and healers. Martyna and Parlo were overjoyed with this arrangement because it allowed them to escape the rigorous regimen of daily life at the temple to more fully explore nature and their own creative energies. Both my parents were well respected as wise beings who were deeply aligned with the truth of the Creator (the creative essence that exists within and around us all).

For me, the first sensations of being held in my mother's and then my father's arms brought forth intense feelings of safety and security as well as a profound awakening within my heart. I felt at home because we had connected as a trinity on the inner planes before my birth; we had planned everything as a united consciousness. My birth was confirmation of our divine plans unfolding on Earth. I remember such things as my birth because the sacred and evolved people present at the time held my energy and awareness open, allowing me to retain all information and relive it, even to this day.

Martyna and Parlo traveled to north Atlantis supported by family and temple members. Upon discovering an expanse of land appropriate for inhabitation, everyone there created from his or her thoughts a home for my parents and me to live in. Nature and its spirits were strong in the north Atlantean countryside, and this made the group's work extremely easy. They first sat together in meditation, calling forth the nature spirits to join them. As their breathing expanded, their bodies relaxed, and their energy vibration increased, allowing them to access a limitless united consciousness in which anything was possible.

Martyna and Parlo projected into the united awareness an image of their ideal home. They saw before them a tree already tall and strong. When they received consent from the tree's essence, they projected an image of a large, circular, wooden home built on many levels with the tree and its branches as the heart of the home. Each person placed the image within the focus of their third eye as if they were viewing the home before them. Collectively activating their heart chakras and emotional bodies, they created a powerful source of light and belief from within, channeling this energy into the image held at their third eye. After a period of focus, a semiphysical home manifested on the land. Everyone then called on the nature spirits to anchor the semiphysical energies into the physical vibration of Earth so that they could vibrate harmoniously. With everyone's continued focus, the large and expansive tree home manifested before our eyes. Even the flowers and vegetables Martyna had imagined appeared fully grown from the soil! Parlo and Martyna especially liked the presence of the tree; they felt it would always protect their energy and remind them how nature's energy physically and spiritually nurtures us all.

In the years that followed, many people moved from the center of Atlantis to the north countryside, creating new villages nestled in nature. A new community of people formed around our home, and Martyna's mother, Amka, a wise priestess, decided to leave temple life behind in exchange for the tranquility and creativity of living close to nature. Parlo's parents, Hamna and Violet, moved from the southern area of central Atlantis to be closer to their growing family. Hamna was a master of the Melchizedek Temple that focused on self-mastery but resigned from his position, choosing a quiet life in the countryside instead. Never before had family life been so important to these people, but as changes occurred within the temples of Atlantis, many retreated to the country to create communities focused only on love in which all people could be themselves and experience their own truth. The strict temple life lost its appeal. However, something more profound was occurring in Atlantis: With each day that passed, it was slowly falling from its high vibrations.

I was extremely grateful to see our community grow from a single home to a village filled with family members and new friends. Each morning, I studied with my Grandmother Amka in the arts of sight beyond Earth and into dimensions. We worked toward advancing my senses, creating and maintaining my lightbody, awakening my chakras, and accessing the truth of my soul group. In the afternoons, I studied with my grandfather, learning to decipher and master disciplining the mind and physical body. We explored the abilities to manifest through thought and to use the body as a malleable vessel for containing light.

My training commenced at the age of three, and at the age of five, I began my instruction with my soul group, the Celestial White Beings, who transported me from my physical reality to their ashram every evening at dusk for an hour. In these times, I discovered and improved my channeling ability of expressing energy, light, and consciousness through every part of my physical body and my voice.

Even before this, Martyna and Parlo taught me the language of the Atlanteans, the priests and priestesses, and the elements. They continued to share sacred languages of the stars and planets, such as Venus, Sirius, and the Pleiades, and when I grow older, the language of the cosmic heart chakra of the universe and the Creator. My parents taught me rituals of cleansing myself and crystals — mantras of protection or light amplification — through fun games that held my focus on the greater purpose of my soul's unfolding on Earth. I was always intrigued to learn new wisdom or practices.

The presence of my beloved friend Jayda filled me with the most happiness each new day as I learned my lesson. There were many children of a similar age who studied with me, and I felt a connection to each, but our intense spiritual instruction led Jayda and me to confide and seek comfort in each other as realizations unfolded from within our beings. We reflected fun, joy, and laughter to each other to maintain a balance of a childlike innocence with our ever-expanding, profound spiritual knowledge at such a young age. Jayda's focus was on the healing vibrations of sound. His favorite instruments were the singing bowls, which even at a tender age he played with great ability and awareness. Jayda, the adults often said, was destined to heal Earth and its people through his knowledge and expression of sound.

In our spare time, Jayda shared some of the sacred chants and tones he discovered. We sat together and sang to whatever would listen, whether it was the flowers or the river. In our younger days, we ran about wildly trying to catch fairies. Our greatest wish was to see a fairy up close. Our game was not imaginary. As colored orbs of light, the fairies encouraged us to run after them. Luckily for them, our attempts at snatching them were feeble. As we grew, we learned to respectfully communicate with the fairies, and our wish was granted. I met my fairy guide, Bluebell, who continues to act as my source of wisdom and my connection with the fairy kingdom, nature spirits, and elementals.

When I was nine, Amka, Hamna, and the Celestial White Beings told my parents that I was ready to achieve my priestess initiations. By this time, I was able to vocally channel the Celestial White Beings, verbally expressing their consciousness. They announced the need for a temple in which they could anchor and express their energies to the people of Atlantis to further aid spiritual awakening and the unification of the people of Atlantis and the Creator. The Celestial White Beings said that they had been training me to protect, anchor, and safeguard their energies, merging their vibration with Earth to allow their presence to manifest on many energetic levels. It was within this temple of the Celestial White Beings, sometimes fondly known as the Temple of Sanctuary by those who visited, that I was to complete my priestess initiations.

As our community gathered to manifest the temple through the power of united consciousness and thought, Hamna and Jayda were appointed by the Celestial White Beings to support the blossoming and further fruition of the temple, the presence of the Celestial White Beings, and my priestess initiations. Hamna played the role of a wise guiding light for me as I adjusted to becoming the guardian and protector of the temple, and Jayda provided constant support and companionship as we explored daily life within the temple. Jayda was also working toward his initiations, as Hamna had been guided to assist him in becoming a Melchizedek master and priest. The temple became a space of sacred learning as Jayda and I began to walk the pathway that had been forecast by our souls.

My life progressed with extreme ease due to the energetic pathways created by the priestesses at my birth. At the age of twenty-two, I became a fully grown Atlantean with long, pale-red hair; a trim athletic body; and a wealth of spiritual understanding. In this phase of my reality, I began to discover my purpose of existing on the plane of Atlantis. In the greater scale of my soul's journey, my Atlantean lifetime was the true beginning of my soul exploration, and it would have a dramatic effect on my lifetimes to come.

I wish to share with you insights into my Atlantean life to assist you in deciphering your own Atlantean past lifetimes, bringing greater understanding and love to your current reality while creating a vast source of compassion and healing for the entire Atlantean civilization. Although I cannot share with you direct insights into central Atlantis temple life, I am aware that my family and I played an important role in the fall of Atlantis — as did you. By sharing my experiences with you, I hope to awaken the Atlantean energy within you once more. The reality many of you experience on Earth now is a continuation of your existence on the plane of Atlantis. It is as if we have waited many lifetimes to now complete what began in Atlantis. Together, let us bring completion to the seeds of ascension planted in Atlantis.

Nara's Notes

As we begin our journey together, it is important that we state our intentions. An intention is a predetermined focus you wish to manifest into an action or experience on Earth. An intention is similar to a goal; it is a purpose you wish to fulfill, however small or large, or a plan you hope to create. Intentions can be born from your mind, emotions, desires, heart, or soul. If born from your mind, emotions, and desires, it may be short-lived, created from a whim or as a result of an experience. Such intentions can be inflexible, causing confusion rather than growth. When an intention forms as a thought or feeling from your heart or soul, it is likely to be truthful, flexible, and appropriate for your greater path and purpose on Earth. Flexibility in your intentions signifies that you do not hold any attachment to your creation while simultaneously holding a concentrated focus.

Your soul, which can be given many names, is the very essence of your being. It is an aspect of the Creator within your being. When wisdom or inspired ideas flow from your soul and intuition, their true purpose is to carry you forward with accuracy in your physical and spiritual reality. If an intention creates the feeling of being blissful, limitless, and expansive, you can be sure it was born from your soul. Once you have grasped your intention, whether it is for the next week or month or year, you are already beginning to manifest the intention within your reality. By adding focus, energy, and enthusiasm to your intention by imagining its current manifestation, you allow yourself to experience it fully. Always carry a focus in your mind fueled with hope, belief, and inner confirmation to assist in your accelerated understanding of yourself and the Creator and to awaken an ability to manifest.

My intentions are to awaken your mind to your Atlantean self, to heal our Atlantean past, to help you reacquire your Atlantean knowledge and skills, and to bring completion and accelerated ascension into your current reality and perspectives on Earth. Will you allow me to fulfill my intention?

I share with you this affirmation that you can use in your daily life to energize our intention:

*I recognize and I am my completely healed Atlantean self. I hold
my Atlantean skills and wisdom as one with my being.*

It is important for you to create and state your own intentions to me
so that I can work with you energetically to assist in their manifestation.
Maybe there is an area of your life you wish to bring healing to, a situation you wish to experience, or an ability you wish to acquire. It could
be that you would like to remember your Atlantean self or access sacred
wisdom that was treasured but lost in Atlantis. Take time to sit in meditation to develop the creation of your intention.

Practice 1
Create Your Intention

Place this book in front of you. Sit with your back straight and your
hands resting on your legs with your palms up. Relax your body as
much as possible as you focus your mind on your breathing.

Inhale deeply into your stomach. Exhale until all the air has
been released. Do this three times.

Bring your focus to your heart chakra at the center of your
chest.

Breathing comfortably, imagine you are inhaling air and
white light through your heart chakra, and exhale with the same
intention. This practice awakens and heals your heart chakra.
It is important to practice breathing through your heart chakra
until it feels natural, maybe for five minutes.

Continue to breathe through your heart chakra as you place
your right hand upon the book and your left hand on your heart.

Say out loud, *I now allow the intention of my soul to rise.*

Wait with patience as your intention, your purpose and goal,
rises from your heart into your mind for your understanding.

It is important to free yourself from doubt and accept the
intention that forms in your mind. Write the intention on a piece
of paper and keep it with this book. In your own time, create an
affirmation that states you are already experiencing your intention.

Practice 2
Connect with Nara

Say out loud,

Beloved Archangel Michael and Archangel Faith, I call on your protection and love to oversee my meditation.

Begin by breathing through your heart chakra until your body and mind feel relaxed. Say out loud,

I open myself as and with the truth of my being from my heart chakra.

Imagine a great release of light from your heart chakra. Say out loud,

Nara Merlyn, I call for your divine guidance and loving support. Surround me in your positive, wise Atlantean light. I am open to a positive, loving connection with you.

I will place before your heart chakra a pure white pearl of light, which represents my soul light. As you inhale, draw the pearl into the center of your heart chakra.

I will place before your third eye chakra at your brow an additional pure white pearl of light representing my soul light. As you inhale, draw the pearl into the center of your third eye chakra.

I stand before you and take hold of your hands, channeling my energy, love, and wisdom into your being. My light flows up your arms and into your heart.

Continue to breathe through your heart chakra, knowing we are creating an eternal connection together and I am sharing with you healing that is needed at this time.

Experience our united energy for as long as you wish, and then send energy from your root chakra at the base of your spine into the earth to ground and center your being once more.

Know that when you are able to feel, sense, or acknowledge my energy in meditation, you can ask me to share wisdom with you, express healing, or awaken energies from within your being. Both of these meditations can be experienced as often as you feel guided to do so.

2

The Temple of the
Celestial White Beings

I created a temple many years ago with the assistance of my guides, the Celestial White Beings, and family members. When it was complete, it stood as a powerful point of anchoring for these pure-consciousness beings and a great source of support for the people of Atlantis. The temple needed to manifest to assist many purposes guided by the will of the Creator. The predominant reasons were to house the light and wisdom and to anchor the presence of the Celestial White Beings.

I, Nara, am a part of the Celestial White Beings' soul group; they are a complete soul group that exists in the cosmic and multi-universal levels of the Creator's universe. Their soul is like a star in the Creator's universe with ashrams; chambers; and a great hall for healing, spiritual awakening, and deeper connection with the Creator's soul. The Celestial White Beings' energy vibrates from the fourteenth dimension of the 144 dimensions, which means that their energy vibrates so fast that it is difficult for them to anchor into Earth's slow vibrational rhythm.

The Celestial White Beings are named so because of their pure white energy. They do not have names or bodies; they simply exist as white light. On their extensive travel to other stars, planets, and dimensions on the inner planes of the Creator's universe, they have collected a great expanse of knowledge that they wish to share with other aspects of the Creator. The Celestial White Beings can appear as a united soul or as thousands of lightbodies, but in truth they are a source of light supporting the spiritual evolution of Earth.

Before my birth as Nara, I was elected to come to Earth as a representative of the Celestial White Beings and to exist in a physical body to help these magnificent beings anchor into the frequencies of Earth. The Celestial White Beings' energy has always been associated with Earth. They gave energy and intention, along with other aspects of the Creator, to facilitate the original manifestation of Earth. With the presence of my temple and my connection to their core soul, the Celestial White Beings were able to anchor into Earth to guide, inspire, and heal many people.

I am an aspect of the Celestial White Beings' source, yet I have not completely accepted that my vibration and essence are the same as theirs. To accept one's soul group takes patience, connection, and devotion. There is a need to explore the energies already manifested within your soul and your soul group to find the bond or link that brings forth realization of unity. The limitations of Earth can encourage us to see ourselves only as physical forms rather than expansive, magnificent sources of light. Through my integration each day with the energy of the Celestial White Beings, I recognize their essence within my being, which stabilizes the blossoming of my conscious awakening as a Celestial White Being on Earth.

Another reason for the temple's manifestation was to house a very sacred crystal — a new feminine crystal — to steady the energy vibration of Atlantis and to store wisdom. This crystal is a double-terminated, clear quartz crystal that is embedded in the domed roof of the temple. Each time the Celestial White Beings anchor their energy into the temple, they pass through the quartz crystal, activating, purifying, and energizing it so that it can continue radiating light across the land of Atlantis. The crystal has a masculine twin, which is anchored in south Atlantis. Created by the high priests and priestesses of Atlantis who dwell in the main cities of the continent, the crystals are part of six sets of twin crystals.

The high priests and priestesses of Atlantis foresaw a lowering in Atlantis's vibration. The remaining crystals were placed in other areas of Earth to assist with the Atlanteans' flight from Atlantis — if need be — as well as to store the wisdom of the Atlantean civilization for future generations. I felt honored to be a guardian of the feminine crystal of Atlantis, even though I knew it was the Celestial White Beings who were its true guardians.

One day, I headed to the temple with Jacob, one of my purest friends. Even though he existed on Earth as a horse, his soul radiated love and enlightenment, which always brought peace to my mind. That day, Jacob's strong legs carried me quickly through the shade of majestic trees as I sat comfortably on his back. He leaped into an expanse of brilliant green meadow, and the blazing sun beat down on us. Jacob continued to canter up the steep landscape, the rhythm of his hooves a constant as he carried me ever forward.

I threw my head back to release the exhilaration within me as feelings of freedom and bliss charged my body with life. Jacob's breathing grew heavier as we reached the steepest part of the hill, but his determination to reach the top drove him onward. A pure white, circular building with a domed roof came into view as we reached the northern coastline of north Atlantis. Jacob shook his head in amusement and pleasure at returning to the temple. Slowing to a gentle trot, he circled the temple many times as if confirming he had reached our destination.

I slid gently from Jacob's back, holding tightly onto his gray mane to steady myself. Lovingly patting his shining coat, I encouraged him to follow me to the cliffside behind the temple. Sitting down as close as I dared to the edge, I felt Jacob standing carefully behind me. Together we gazed out to sea, breathing in the fresh, salty air to purify our auras. The sea was calm and turquoise blue. This was one of my favorite places to sit and meditate, and I had been visiting it since I was a young girl. I was always fascinated by the majestic presence of the sea — sometimes energizing, other times mellow in its influence on my being. But the sea couldn't entice me today, because my thoughts were with the tall, gray horse standing close behind me. I sensed Jacob would be leaving me and Earth soon.

Jacob had been my wonderful companion for two years. I originally befriended him after finding him wandering near the temple. He began to return to the temple regularly and even communicated telepathically with me. On several occasions, I was able to guide him into the temple to receive healing.

I knew Jacob would soon ascend. He would leave behind his physical body to exist as pure white light, becoming a unicorn. I had heard of many horses on Atlantis who had achieved a high volume of light within their physical bodies that allowed them to ascend and become unicorns on the inner planes or dimensions of the Creator's universe. I had become a part of Jacob's ascension on the day we met, and ever since, I had helped him access the light within himself, absorb more life force energy, and quicken his energetic vibration.

As I turned to look up at Jacob, I was aware of the energetic unicorn horn protruding from his third eye chakra at his brow. A unicorn's horn is a spiraling light from the being's soul that manifests through the third eye, enhancing its abilities to manifest, create magic, and see through dimensions with tremendous clarity. Jacob and I had finished resolving his past issues of abandonment by exploring the energies, thoughts, and memories he held on to, so I knew he would soon be ready to return to the inner planes.

"Jacob," I said as I rummaged in my pocket to produce a crystal heart with a golden hue, "I know you are leaving soon, so I wanted to gift you this crystal as a thank you for your friendship. Maybe I could plait it into your mane?"

Jacob's eyes pierced deeply into my own. "I will soon return home, leaving the physical land behind. I am now ready to be your guide, Nara, from the inner planes, energetically walking with you each day and entering your circle of guides who support your life on Earth. It is a great honor for me; a new part of my spiritual evolution is dawning. I will become closer to you and to the Creator, recognizing my skills and abilities more fully. Do not grieve me when I take my last breath on Earth, because I will be given far more than could possibly be experienced here. I still have some time yet. I thank you, Nara, for your gift of the crystal heart."

As Jacob's words faded in my mind, he lowered his energy horn to the crystal I held up to him. He inhaled with focus and then exhaled, sending a beam of light through the crystal and directly into my third eye chakra. My mind's attentions instantly became internal. The crystal was energetically forming within my mind, its light washing over every thought of my present, past, and future. My mind relaxed as if it were sighing in relief. My grief for Jacob melted away, leaving a feeling of bliss. We existed in unison for some time as the presence of the crystal became stronger in my awareness.

"Nara, I have anchored into your mind all the loving qualities and thoughts that I recognize within myself. This way, you will always be connected to my consciousness and soul." Jacob's kind words drifted gently through my mind.

"Thank you," was all I could offer in return. I sensed Jacob retreat as I continued to process my experience. Unaware of time's passing, I explored the expanse of my mind.

When I felt ready, I stood and turned to face my temple. Walking around to the front, I opened the door to the brilliant white room bathed in sunlight. I was surprised to see no one was using the temple. Normally, I would find people sitting with their backs against the temple's curved wall in deep meditation and connection with the Celestial White Beings or the Creator. The volume of people visiting the temple from the main cities had declined, but many still came to connect with the feminine crystal or because they had heard of the healing and ascension advancement that the Celestial White Beings assisted. The high priests and priestesses from the main temples in Atlantis often encouraged their students to visit my temple because they honored the wisdom that the Celestial White Beings radiated. The location of the temple denoted it as a place of sanctuary surrounded by luscious green nature land and constantly purified and protected by the salty sea air.

Although my mind was still pulsating with the golden light Jacob had anchored as a gift of friendship and connection with his soul, I felt a great urgency to sit and accept the energy of the Celestial White Beings.

"Beloved Celestial White Beings, I open my channel and consciousness to you. I ask you to descend into the temple so that we may connect as one." My voice echoed with power in the domed ceiling.

The mammoth quartz crystal above me began to vibrate, sending shudders through the white stone walls into the soil of Atlantis. My breathing became extremely expansive, and my mind followed the gentle rhythm of my breath. With my awareness shifting away from my body and the room I was in, I became aware of the Celestial White Beings gathering in a translucent ring of light. Images of tall lightbodies bobbing gently and radiating such blissful love seeped into my mind. The Celestial White Beings had arrived! Their light flowed into every chakra within my being, charging me with their consciousness.

"Nara Merlyn, we wish to anchor energy through your being into the land of Atlantis to support an increase in energy vibration," the Celestial White Beings shared with love.

I understood their request perfectly, as I had been working closely with Celestial White Beings for seventeen year. Their vibration — although familiar — was always inspirational to connect with. I sent a thought of activation to the eight human-sized clear crystal points that had been embedded in the floor of the temple with half their form exposed. Their points faced out from the center of the temple to create a star-like channel for the light to be amplified and cast in all directions across the land of Atlantis and the sea. The floor of the temple trembled as the crystals responded to my thought.

Altering the pattern of my breathing, I began to inhale and focus on drawing light down through my crown chakra into my heart chakra. As I exhaled, I allowed the white light to be absorbed into every cell and molecule of my being and auric field. Inhaling once more, I drew the light through my crown chakra, down my spine, and into a chakra below my feet known as the earth star chakra. Exhaling, I imagined the light flowing into the eight crystals and being transmitted into the land and people of Atlantis. Repeating this pattern of focus, I was aware of the power created by anchoring the light and consciousness of the Celestial White Beings into my earth star chakra. It allowed for all energies to manifest by entering the physical vibration of Earth and becoming true and present in the physical reality.

I sat for what seemed like only a few minutes but was actually a few hours, shifting my consciousness and awareness to achieve a greater communion with the light of the Celestial White Beings, feeding my soul with an experience of oneness and expansive knowledge. My body was becoming so filled with light that it felt as if I were floating, suspended in clouds of whiteness. Through my efforts of existing as an anchor for the Celestial White Beings, they were connecting with many people on Atlantis to offer guidance, wisdom, inspiration, healing, and inner strength. They were able to achieve energetic shifts within the structure and vibration of Earth with support from the archangels. I always enjoyed these moments of Earth healing and shifts, as I truly experienced the connection of complete love between the Celestial White Beings and the archangels for the people of Atlantis.

My experience of oneness with the people of Atlantis increased. It was as if they were aware of the light that was radiating and opened themselves to receive it. Archangel Michael and his feminine manifestation, Archangel Faith, drew close to support me at these times. Archangel Michael was my main guide overseeing my channel, spiritual education, and protection.

It always amazed me to watch as he led the archangels in the light-weaving process, when wisdom and light combine and interlace to create what can only be described as a blanket of light woven into the energy vibration of Earth. Light weaving achieved by the archangels allows humanity to absorb necessary understanding to create the divine plan of the Creator on Earth.

Impressions of gratitude and completion seeped into my mind, signifying the end of the healing and energy-transference session. I began to inhale, drawing energy up from the earth. My exhale sent the light of my being back into the earth as a practice of grounding myself in my physical reality.

"We wish to enlighten your mind and fill your soul with wisdom." The Celestial White Beings merged their consciousness with my mind. "Imagine the pale pink rose in your heart expanding and sharing love openly and limitlessly, as we have taught you before. Allow yourself, Nara, to be conscious and accepting of our guidance. Imagine our energy is entering the rose while activating wisdom its the very core. This way, you are always in a process of receiving and providing for yourself from your soul." My heart felt as if it would explode with the intensity of love growing within it.

"In the presence of love," the Celestial White Beings instructed, "we wish to share with you that the vibration of Atlantis is continuing to decline. We and many lightbeings on Earth and the inner planes are sending tremendous volumes of light into the earth to support an awakening and realization of what is truly occurring. You might have noticed we have been asking you to anchor more light and consciousness into the earth; we truly wish to awaken humanity to realizations of truth before a pathway unfolds that could cause learning and spiritual growth to take place through the forms of chaos, challenges, and fear in future generations and civilizations on Earth. The people of Atlantis are being asked to dissolve the energetic patterns of fear, separation, and inner chaos that were created in the previous two civilizations of Atlantis. Now is the time to dissolve the karmic patterns created so that they no longer repeat in other lifetimes. The intentions and decisions you make in this lifetime determine your experiences in later lives. You cannot be free from their creation unless you actively and consciously choose to release and let go of energetic habits and patterns, shifting your mind's focus to create new intentions of higher vibrations."

The Celestial White Beings' words brought a wave of guilt and self-contemplation into my mind as I considered whether I had evaluated my own karmic patterns and habits of fear with the dedication that was required. My thoughts were pushed aside as the Celestial White Beings continued their channeling through me.

"Let us remind you of the fear, manipulations, and suppression that your parents experienced in central Atlantis before your birth. Your parents' purpose of building a family and community here was a guided attempt to be free from growing energetic restrictions in order to hold the light of the Creator strong within many to be used as a powerful force of healing. As light is created in the outskirts and countryside of Atlantis, it is easily magnified by nature, creating a balance and opposing healing to the growing presence of suppression. As the light of the Creator grows strong in many, it weaves a powerful force through the fog of negativity to enlighten and awaken hearts and souls to the truth of the Creator once more."

Intense light visions filled my mind, causing my brow to furrow with concentration as my third eye chakra and mind worked hard to decipher the meaning of the images. The consciousness that downloaded from the Celestial White Beings into my mind and was expressed through my voice quickened.

"The priests and priestesses of some of the central temples of Atlantis, once of pure and loving intention, are now becoming overshadowed and receptive to negative, controlling vibrations that are entering the atmosphere of Earth. These vibrations are coming from the universe and from misguided souls on Earth who chose separation and technological advancements rather than oneness with the Creator, community, love, and divine connection.

"The ego is growing within many, as they perceive they are beyond the council of their guides and souls, being fueled now only by greed for power. It is time for all Atlantean people to let go of the material experiences, objects, technology, and greed to create a space for truth, peace, and healing. We can only share our light vibrations to open hearts like gentle pink roses to the sunlight; however, the wielding and experience of fear is becoming too strong in its hold over some people of Atlantis. Soon opportunities will flow forward, asking each person to make a choice that will influence the evolution of the Creator's soul that is eternally on Earth.

"Remember, Nara, you and humanity are actively experiencing in order to boost the evolution of the Creator, the universe, and All That Is. Each one of you is an aspect of the Creator; you walk as the humble, loving vibration of the Creator to achieve unity, realization, and an expansive awareness of truth, which allows the source of the Creator to be energized with complete abundance and vibrational elevation within you. Everything achieved now is for a higher purpose, often beyond your comprehension, to create a greater abundance of life. It is time to come back to the abundance of source and life within rather than create abundance in the extremities of your being and reality — without the inner core activated. This will only create a lowering of vibration, confusion in the mind, and separation from the constant flow of the Creator that naturally feeds and nurtures your being, whether you exist on Earth, the inner planes, or the central heart chakra of the Creator.

"Nara, to be in the flow of the Creator's energy is to cocreate each moment with the Creator. To separate yourself or to consciously disconnect from the eternal flow is to starve yourself and your soul, causing pain and suffering. The light we share through you now is offering to Atlanteans a conscious realization of their actions so that an internal decision can be made. Will Atlanteans choose love and unity, which have always been present as a seed in their hearts, or will they choose fear and separation as additions to the outer world and the advancement of growing technology? Dear souls of Earth, we have been at this junction many a time. We ask you to return to oneness."

The Celestial White Beings' plea to humanity lingering in the air, and I felt the energy of the temple shift as these magnificently loving beacons of light withdrew their energy. I entered back into the reality of the white temple with its hard, cold marble floor.

I tingled with delight as energy crawled over and through my body, and I reflected on the words of the Celestial White Beings. It was a message I had heard many times, warning humanity — and even myself, I realized — of the choices and creations we make and how we can influence all forms of reality. For me, the reality of fear, suppression, and manipulation seemed unlikely; however, I had never visited any other area of Atlantis. The community I experienced in my daily life was one of joy, love, sharing, and encouragement. Community and unity were extremely important to us and had become the foundation of each person's spiritual awakening, especially my own. We had manifested much to serve us as a community, even the beautiful temple I resided in now.

People from other parts of Atlantis often visited the temple and shared stories of how machines and controlling devices were being built or that many people were becoming embedded in fear and were unable to escape its hold. There was talk that the crystals within the energy matrix of Atlantis were being charged with negative consciousness and dark magic to deplete the light of each soul. I realized that to believe the stories was to play a part in cocreating their presence on Earth, so I chose to view Atlantis as a beacon of love that all could tap into and experience fully. Maybe that could be perceived as naive, but a belief or perspective is a powerful tool to influence the entire reality of Earth, and I chose to stay in my power.

As a priestess still learning and evolving with each day, I chose my power to be love. My tool to wield my power was my ability to choose my actions, thoughts, and reality while supported and advised by my guides and soul. Do you believe you have the freedom to wield your power of love through your ability to choose and take action?

Nara's Notes

When guidance and intuition warn and advise you in connection with certain situations in your reality or on Earth, remain in your power. There is a need to remain centered within your being, to focus on yourself as a beacon of love and on your conscious expression of love. To remain in your power and to choose love as your power create a sacred space where creation of anything needed can be achieved in balance and clarity. You then have the strength to wield your power with choice as your tool, allowing you to accept or discard according to your inner truth and essence.

To view yourself as an equal to your guides is not prohibited as long as it flows as knowingness within rather than as an egocentric belief. The energy and advice of your guides hold a certain amount of importance, as they are able to currently view a greater expanse of all the opportunities available to you.

It is essential that you find a balance among what you wish to create, the guidance shared, and the action you need to take in your reality and on behalf of Earth. You are then able to walk through your reality with ease, understanding pathways that could distract you and lower your vibrations while considering pathways that will lead to greater evolvement. Observing the wisdom shared with and activated within you is always a tool, as it promotes further clarity within the mind and heart and allows a pathway of ease to unfold. The more you and every person around you evolves, the more it becomes essential to remain in your own energy and to observe all aspects of the Creator that are unfolding. That way, you will not be influenced by the presence and beliefs of others unless you choose to be.

It is with this consciousness in mind that I wish to assist your connection with the Celestial White Beings, who want to be of service to you. Their greatest abilities are cleansing and healing, stripping away all unneeded energies and untruths from your being to encourage you to view the beautiful essence of your self and your origins. Like a breath of fresh air, the Celestial White Beings raise your energy vibration, pouring light into your being to bring greater illumination and enlightenment on many levels. Their energetic vibrations are of multiuniversal and cosmic levels resembling the Creator quality of bliss. When bliss is achieved in all energetic bodies and aspects of our beings, then we completely exist in oneness with the Creator. Oneness with all that is the Creator is the ultimate goal of ascension, as it signifies you exist eternally in the expansive flow and energy of the Creator, accessing all abilities and skills available to be of service to others.

Practice 3
Connect with the Celestial White Beings

You might want to call on the energies of the Celestial White Beings to draw close to you during meditation or quiet time. Their energies can be extremely intense, causing drowsiness or the experience of a current of energy flowing through your body. Each person's experience of the Celestial White Beings' energy will be different as they work uniquely alongside your soul to make necessary shifts within to further awaken your awareness of truth. When calling on the Celestial White Beings, it is important to allow space and time for their light to work with you as needed.

A beautiful mantra that aligns your entire being to the vibration of the Celestial White Beings is *Om Na*, which translates to, "I am bliss." A wonderful practice is to repeat, "Om Na, I am bliss" in your mind or out loud in meditation for five to ten minutes. This will act as a sound vibration to call the Celestial White Beings to work closely with you, pouring their vibration of bliss into your being to activate experiences of bliss from within. Repeating the mantra "Om Na, I am bliss" in your mind as you go about your daily routine will enhance the quality of bliss within your energetic field while developing your connection with the Celestial White Beings, an aspect of the Creator.

Practice 4
Pale-Pink Rose of Giving and Receiving

Sit peacefully, focusing on relaxing your physical body as you follow the rhythm of your breath with your mind.

Imagine a pale-pink rose in your heart chakra in the center of your chest. Allow yourself to observe or sense the rose, noticing how alive the rose is with energy. Witness how the light and petals of it expand as you exhale and how the rose is nurtured and energized with every breath you inhale.

The rose symbolizes your ability to openly and limitlessly share love while consciously accepting guidance activated from within, or given as it flows into the rose, thus supporting your recognition of your inner power. Say out loud,

I call on Archangel Michael to protect and oversee my connection with the Celestial White Beings. I call on the Celestial White Beings to lovingly draw close, embracing me completely in your blissful light. Please work alongside my soul to promote greater healing, spiritual awakening, the presence of truth, and an increase in my energy vibration. I ask you to assist me in whatever way divinely serves me in this moment. I open myself up in acceptance and expression of the Creator. Thank you.

Imagine a pure white light flowing from all directions deep into the rose at your heart chakra. Allow yourself to be conscious and accepting of any guidance or healing the Celestial White Beings wish to share. As you receive energy, you are simultaneously activating wisdom from the very core of the rose. This way, you are always in a process of receiving and providing for yourself from your soul.

Sit for as long and as often as you wish when you connect with the Celestial White Beings. With patience, your connection will develop.

CHAPTER

3

Self-Discovery within Unity

After a brisk walk down the hill from the temple in the warm night air, I arrived at my parents' house. Their tree house, now surrounded by many other homes built over the years as the community evolved, was the central point of a very special gathering tonight. The moon shone brightly onto our humble community, signifying it was the gathering for the full moon celebration. A hive of activity, sound, and energy was emanating from behind the tree house as everyone gathered together in the garden to celebrate, rejoice, and connect with a focus of unity. The full moon, to us, signified a new energetic cycle within our realities and beings. We celebrated the release of the old and the acceptance of the new higher vibrations of light from the universe that blessed us daily. We recognized the Moon as a symbol of wholeness, of unity, of oneness, so we were guided to gather when the full moon was present to aid our connection with the Creator and each other. Our energies became heightened and sensitive at this time, allowing us to delve deeper into our Creator aspect within.

Parlo always organized the full moon celebrations. He found it easy to connect with each soul present, encouraging a feeling of comfort and coaxing the space to expand the heart chakra more fully. With his outgoing personality and beaming smile, he encouraged all to be at one within their hearts so that immense healing and heart awakening could take place as they bathed in the light of the moon.

As I turned the corner into the garden, I was met by a warm wave of laughter and joy. I was later than I thought, and already more than a hundred people had gathered, drinking and eating and sharing their beautiful stories while laughing as loudly as their hearts desired.

"Beloved Nara, my beautiful daughter, welcome to the night of the heart awakening and Creator light bathing!" Parlo greeted me with the same love he exuded to each being. His heart was open to express and receive with abundance.

"Are you well tonight, Parlo?" I asked, smiling warmly.

"Yes, yes, yes! I am excited, as Jayda has granted us a healing sound session tonight, which has brought many new people to gather with us."

Parlo was bouncing with energy; it was his favorite evening of the month. He enjoyed preparing for the celebration as well as the celebration itself. The garden had been furnished with tables, chairs, cushions, candles, crystals, and brightly colored ribbons intertwined through the branches of the surrounding trees. I delighted at the spectacle as my father moved to greet new arrivals.

Scanning the party, I searched for familiar faces. First Ted and Marie caught my eye. Ted was my mother's brother — identical in features, with curly red hair that he kept short, pale skin, and rosy red lips. Ted towered over Marie even though she was one of the taller ladies in our community. Marie often appeared timid, yet she was divinely serene and tremendously peaceful, which manifested as a dazzling beauty that enhanced her somewhat plain features. Like my mother, Ted had been a member of the central temples in Atlantis. He met Marie when he moved to the countryside, following his sister to a greater space of sanctuary. Marie had followed the guidance of her soul, which led her all the way from southern Atlantis as she searched for her soul mate for this lifetime. Her heart was strong and wise, guiding her to where she needed to be for her divine plan to unfold further. Ted and Marie married in the Celestial White Beings' temple, where they opened their hearts in true love to each other with the entire community and the Creator as their witnesses.

At the far end of the garden, I spotted my grandmother, Amka. Her long, gray hair, once fiery-red like her children's, tumbled and swayed against her small, slight body as she excitedly spoke to a tall young man. Amka, eighty-seven years old in physical years, still held the muscular strength of a forty-year-old. Although she was obviously offering council to the young man who seemed deeply engrossed in her words, I couldn't stop myself and ran across the garden to greet her. It had been a while since I had seen Amka, as she was always busy tutoring the children of our community. Her back was to me, so I gently placed my hand on her right shoulder. My heart filled with joy as she turned her entire body in anticipation of me enfolding her in my arms. Pushing her away slightly, I gazed into her wise, gray eyes, feeling her love stream back to me.

"Nara, I would like you to meet Benjamin, who will be staying with me for a while, as he feels guided to draw on my knowledge." Amka looked affectionately up at the young man she'd been talking to. It seemed as if she could clearly see the young man's destiny, and she delighted in the role she would play in its manifestation.

Peeling my gaze from my grandmother, I observed the man before me. His pale-blue eyes drew me in as if I were looking into the depths of his soul. All I saw was white light, so pure and beautiful — like the ocean in constant movement. Benjamin was muscular, and his long brown hair was neatly tied back. He smiled at me with the same knowingness I recognized from Amka, which instantly put me at ease while causing questions of wonder to fill my mind. Parlo's sudden announcement to the gathering interrupted further communication with Amka and Benjamin.

As I turned, I saw Jayda's handsome, tanned face beaming amid a gathering of people who quickly moved into what seemed the perfect space for them to enjoy the evening session. Jayda sat cross-legged in the center. His golden hair blew gently in the light wind against his muscular shoulders. Jayda was tall and strong while his heart and energy vibration were gentle and beautifully loving. He always seemed so laid-back, regardless of what was occurring around or within him. A powerful innocence exuded from his heart at all times. Wearing a pure white robe, he projected tranquility in the moment as he energetically linked into the vibration of the five white crystal bowls that encircled him. Serenity moved through the audience as Jayda aligned with the crystal vibration of the singing bowls and transmitted it through his channel and heart chakra to all who were willing to receive.

I quickly found a space, and my heart opened extensively from the simple presence of Jayda. Our connection was so strong and pure that my heart sent pearls of white light to his heart in response to the love he radiated.

"Sending you divine blessings this evening, Jayda," I telepathically transmitted, instantly feeling his response of love.

"Beloved Nara, you are in my heart this evening," he telepathically returned.

As I closed my eyes, I glimpsed Jayda lift his baton to begin to share the vibrational sound of the crystal singing bowls. Waves of exquisite sounds filled the night sky as Jayda brought into our reality not only a healing vibrational sound but also a sacred transmission of the crystal consciousness of the inner planes.

Each crystal on Earth holds a consciousness, or energy vibration, that is borne from the crystalline kingdom on the inner planes and is akin to a soul aspect of the Creator. The crystal consciousness vibration slows in order for crystals to manifest at a physical level. Each crystal is a gift of magnification, purification, and sacred connection to All That Is — the Creator. While different crystals hold unique qualities, each crystal has the ability to energetically or consciously transport a soul into the universe of the Creator.

Jayda continued to radiate sound and energy from every cell of his being. Although he sat strongly grounded to the earth, he was present with each person, energetically promoting and supporting their individual healing.

As strong healing vibrations washed over and through me, I felt Jayda's energetic form gently support me in his arms. The warmth of his heart, like a soft pink blanket, enveloped me as Archangel Michael and the angelic kingdom drew close to surround us both.

"My beloved Nara, the angels and I ask you to bring forth your soul essence to us tonight. Do not be fearful, for you are surrounded in my love and healing vibration. Let your soul penetrate all levels of illusion, entering your heart and physical being with more magnificence and abundance than ever before. My beloved priestess, I — Jayda, your lifelong friend — am here as a representative of the love you hold within your being and soul. Now is the time to allow your soul's power to step into your being as you experience an intense new soul awakening and integration. Your soul's power, the power of the Celestial White Beings, is required to be transmitted through your being into your cells to support your forthcoming experiences on Earth. Accept your power, and you will accept your truth and be able to assist Atlantis in greater ways. I know you well, Nara. The time you have been waiting for to be of greater assistance to all has come. Let yourself feel the true awakening and transmission of your soul with my support as you move into your true identity at a physical level."

I felt myself melt into Jayda's energetic presence, surrendering all I experienced myself to be in the moment as if setting myself free from the burdens of a physical body and life in the earthly dimensions. Jayda's energy, accompanied by the surrounding angelic vibrations, penetrated through the chambers of my heart chakra as a driving force of light, moving through and expanding my heart chakra. As if in miniature, I saw a vision of Jayda and me existing together within a golden chamber of light in the very core of my heart space. Brilliant love radiated from our beings as we connected deeply within my heart.

"It is time to heal the past in order for your soul to step forward into greater embodiment to proceed along your sacred path." Jayda's words touched a deep sensitivity within my being and awakened a vision in my awareness.

It was a vision I was very familiar with: A timeline unfolded that began with Jayda declaring his love for me and his wish to remain with me eternally as we sat with our backs against the white wall outside the temple, gazing at the setting sun as it moved beyond the horizon of the sea. Bliss, joy, and fulfillment filled my being once more as I accessed my memory. Then the timeline continued without my permission, transporting my mind to a scene of Jayda and me crouched together on the temple floor. He had learned from his guides that he was to partner with a woman from the village named Leesha to fulfill his soul's purpose on Earth. This partnership meant he could no longer devote his love to me and would relinquish his duties at the temple.

Dismay, heartbreak, and pain filled the atmosphere as we questioned the cruelty of the Creator in separating us after a lifetime of connection and oneness. All projections we had created for our future together hung as tainted portraits in our minds of what would never come to pass. The timeline ushered me forward into a final memory, and I saw myself lying lifeless on the temple floor, alone with the coldness of that floor as it numbed my physical body and felt more inviting than the presence of the Celestial White Beings. Emotions had been activated within me through this experience that I had never sensed before, feelings that were so overwhelming that all my wisdom as a priestess felt useless.

"Nara, we have come so far since these memories. We have both healed ourselves and restored our faith in each other and the Creator. Although we cannot be together in this lifetime, we know our hearts and souls are always one, and we can only hope our souls will choose to reincarnate on Earth, allowing us to share a full lifetime together. I remind you of these times because there is one final act that needs to be achieved to free your soul expression. That which blocks the soul is different for every person; however, it is often focused on a lack of love or of self-love. Nara, there is a need for you to dissolve all attachment to me to fully and completely heal and love yourself unconditionally. The love we hold for each other cannot be diminished, as love is the presence of the Creator and is eternal. It serves us to dissolve all attachments so that we no longer influence each other energetically and can bring completion to our individual journeys."

With Jayda's words, I allowed the healing to take place. Surrounded by light, I felt myself being lifted up and my heart chakra emanating light as it powerfully began to restore itself. I experienced a deep love and gratitude for my soul, all I was on Earth and the inner planes. Love filled my consciousness and senses, carrying me on a journey of deeper inner peace than I'd ever experienced before. I realized unconditional, humble love for the self is all that is required, and it can bring forth healing on many levels.

"With this realization, you are healed, clearing a space for your soul to be more fully active within your being," Jayda confirmed.

Opening my eyes, I found my surroundings peaceful. Jayda had completed his sound healing session, and the gathered people were emerging from their meditative states with expressions of bliss. Jayda's hand reached down to pull me from the ground. His smile was vibrant as his eyes shimmered with light.

"Do you feel healed?" he whispered in my ear.

"You were conscious of what just happened between us?" I asked, slightly taken aback. Looking into Jayda's eyes, I knew something powerful and guided had just occurred for both of us.

"These bowls now belong to you." Jayda gestured to the five white crystal singing bowls ranging in size from small to large. "It was your healing, Nara. The bowls will continue your healing, aiding your soul to be in action within your body with greater power. You will find them in your temple tomorrow morning."

I gazed in amazement and gratitude at Jayda and then the crystal singing bowls.

Parlo's voice cut through the sound of the gathered people discussing their experiences. "It's time to complete our full moon celebration in the traditional way."

Everyone formed a large circle holding hands. Jayda quickly grasped my right hand, and I was surprised to see Benjamin reaching for my left.

"Bless you all. This is a gathering of love, with energies shared and inner lights enhanced. Feel the energy that runs through your body flowing from hand to hand, creating a connection and union as we stand in the presence of the moon. We call on Goddess Moon to bathe our sacred bodies in the blissful vibrations of the Moon and the universe. We demonstrate to the Creator our readiness to work as one with each other and for the universe to aid the return of the one true spirit within our beings. We are grateful for the blessings and guidance bestowed on us throughout the past month as we open our heart chakras to receive the gifts, guidance, and protection from the universe for the coming month ahead. Let all that is provided to you now from the Moon, the universe, and the Creator abundantly emanate throughout your entire being as you hold the intention of generously sharing all you receive with the beloved souls of our united circle. Thank you." Parlo's words completed the full moon celebration.

I felt such an energetic surge flowing through my body. It was as if every part of me was being energized with light. My left palm chakra burned with intensely expanding light, and as the sensation subsided, I experienced a growing weight in my hand — as if Benjamin were leaning toward me. Opening my eyes, I was surprised to see Benjamin was no longer beside me. As I uncurled my fingers, I glimpsed a light-engraved symbol on my palm of a golden triangle, disk, and serpent imprinted on top of each other. I gazed in wonder as the symbol shined with brightness from my skin.

"That is your soul symbol." Amka's wise voice cut through my surprise. She stood closely to me, whispering into my ear as if she were sharing the most sacred secret. "At your birth, the priestesses engraved your soul symbol into your palm chakras with light. They understood from reading your soul plan that one of your soul's intentions for this lifetime was to meet with a soul from the same soul group as you. Through this soul-symbol light engraving, they offered you a tool to recognize the being from your soul group with greater ease."

"Are you speaking of a soul mate, Amka?" My whisper was so small that Amka only smiled knowingly, revealing no more as she kissed my cheek and walked away.

Nara's Notes

Accepting healing and allowing yourself to move through shifts of realizations to achieve deep, healing transformations are part of your self-discovery process on Earth. Each realization or intention of letting go of what you hold on to and what might be hindering the greater presence of your soul is a mammoth step forward to connect with and experience the light of the Creator within your being. Remember that every pain, uncomfortable feeling, or thought is a beautiful and positive opportunity for you to become more complete in your expression of the Creator. Your soul gradually merges with your entire being over time with your self-inspection; the integration isn't an instantaneous experience but more so a process of your recognizing the presence of your soul within you. As you remove false energy from within, you allow yourself to glimpse your soul, and in doing so, you create a deeper unity and oneness with the Creator.

You might discover every obstruction, pain, or hindrance within you originates in a lack of love, symbolizing that through your unconditional love for yourself, you can gain enlightenment and an awareness of the consciousness of the Creator. To show unconditional self-love is to hold a space of humble love within and around yourself, thinking, acting, reacting, and existing from the natural source of love within your being. Think of yourself in loving ways to constantly dissolve aspects of your ego, allowing judgments, false ideas, and fears to fall away.

Loving yourself unconditionally allows you not only to honor yourself but also to recognize the same space of love within all. Viewing those around you as beacons of love, even when they do not act in this way, assists you in accessing the unity of the Creator. It helps you realize everything and everyone holds the presence of the Creator and are interconnected as an expanded network of light that extends from the source of the Creator.

Practice 5
Encourage Self-Love

Self-love is the key to accessing the divinity, sacred vibrations, and wisdom of your being. It can support you in dissolving all unneeded attachments.

Place both hands on your heart chakra in the center of your chest as you focus on breathing deeply.

Inhale deeply as you say in your mind, "I am love."

Exhale deeply as you say in your mind, "I love myself unconditionally."

Notice the feeling of love activating within your heart chakra as you use your breath as a tool to encourage love to expand into your entire being. Practice this for ten minutes until it feels comfortable, and then extend the time if you feel guided to do so.

This is a healing practice that is particularly influential in times of sadness, distress, lack of confidence, or emotional pain. It will also assist a deep healing within your being, whether conscious or unconscious, aiding you in accessing new levels of self-awareness.

Practice 6
Erase Lack of Love

Erasing lack of love can become a lifelong journey as you constantly access new layers of your own energies while healing past-life memories held within your soul. Focusing on the love of your being will support your embodiment of love. Where there is love, darkness and negativity cannot exist; thus, your entire being will embark on a natural healing process as you return to the origin of your being: love.

Sit peacefully, focusing on your breathing until you feel centered and attentive. Say out loud,

My beloved soul, please bring my attention now to areas of my being or reality where I continue to hold on to and reinforce lack of love. Thank you.

Simply be observant of your thoughts. Memories, past experiences, visions, or inspiration might come to the surface of your mind. Be patient with yourself and trust in what emerges in your mind. Sometimes the realization emerges as a feeling or knowingness from within your being. Be conscious of any energies that activate.

Your purpose is to recognize when you lack in love for yourself and others. You are then able to heal the situation, memory, or realization by returning love to yourself. Say out loud,

I erase all lack of love within my being and reality. I choose to bathe myself in a pure love from my soul and the Creator, restoring the power of love within my being. I am love, and I love myself unconditionally. I am now healed in the presence of love. Thank you.

Imagine love in the form of light flowing from your heart into every aspect of your body, especially to the areas, feelings, or realizations you have been focusing on. Give yourself as much time as is required to fully experience this healing. You might find yourself using this technique often as your love flows more fully, illuminating any lack of love you might be holding on to.

Practice 7
Awaken the Moon

The Moon is a powerful source of Creator energy with the ability to activate and clear much from within your being. On a full moon, allow yourself to stand before the moon, gazing at its luminosity. Say out loud,

I honor the Goddess Moon, calling on her guidance and love to surround me. I ask the Goddess Moon to awaken my soul's luminosity, my body's vitality and vigor, my mind's crystal clear clarity, and the purity of my emotions. Assist me in experiencing a deep cleansing to release all that is no longer needed as you restore my entire being to a quicker vibration of light. As I receive the Goddess Moon, I receive the Creator and my soul, experiencing a unity and oneness to strengthen my being. I open myself to receive the divine gifts and blessings of the universe as they unfold throughout the coming month. Thank you.

Let yourself breathe the luminosity of the moon into every cell of your being as you focus on your intention.

CHAPTER

4

Soul Sounding

Crystalline sounds swelled, filling the circular temple in a swirling crescendo as I lifted the baton away from the largest crystal singing bowl. Jayda's crystal singing bowls had awaited my arrival at the temple the next morning, and I was instantly enthused with an overwhelming desire to play each one, starting with the smallest and moving successively up to the largest, allowing my senses to appreciate each vibrational sound. The sounds activated my soul and expanded my heart, and my soul star chakra above my head felt as if it were beaming a powerful spotlight on my being. Higher aspects of my soul entered through my soul star chakra and were transmitted into my entire being.

The Celestial White Beings taught me to use my heart chakra as a gateway of expression and radiance for my soul because it was a pure space that could be trusted and was less influenced by the ego. It is always important to be aware of your earth star chakra below your feet, as this holds a direct connection to your soul star chakra; one cannot be activated without the other. The earth star chakra acts as a grounding point for the soul, materializing the soul into physical manifestation within your being.

Jayda said the bowls would continue my healing and my greater integration with my soul. Holding this intention, I placed my conscious awareness into my heart chakra, connecting with my soul presence. Great luminosity filled my mind as I felt a stirring of energy rise from my heart into my throat. A powerful tone escaped from my mouth: "Om," the eternal sound of the universe, vibrated throughout the temple. My soul was expressing itself through my voice, distributing its vibration beyond my heart chakra.

"*Om Na Ka Ta Ma Ra*," I began to repeat automatically as a sacred rhythm unfolded from my soul. It was the sound of my soul corresponding to its name.

The Celestial White Beings entered the temple and embraced me in their energy. Their consciousness began to stream into my mind: "You are channeling your soul, Nara. You are channeling our energy — more importantly, the aspect of our energy you represent. Let the sound flow with freedom from your being. As you physically create the sound of your soul, which vibrates eternally within its core, you bring it into physical manifestation on Earth."

I invited the Celestial White Beings to energize and enhance all I was achieving and experiencing. The energies around and within me began to escalate as I felt myself drift deeper into the presence of my soul. A vision of myself as a white glowing being with hints of pink, blue, and gold imprinted into my mind. I was formless, and yet I recognized the vision as myself. Images from simultaneous lifetimes emerged from my soul form to demonstrate the diversity and many aspects, or qualities, of my soul. All were relevant and created the soul I was familiarizing myself with once more. I realized the soul I connected with was a combination of all my experiences on Earth, the planets, the stars, and the inner planes, while also being the purest vibration or example of my soul group.

Colorful characters danced around me, demonstrating their skills and abilities. A Native American Indian girl shook her long black hair as she turned to face me, drawing her bow and arrow taut as her eyes penetrated mine. The name May Flower flowed into my mind. The girl's fierce focus vanished as she transformed into a wolf and disappeared into the distance. A beautiful, innocent girl with blond hair knelt in her white robes holding a golden chalice. She spoke her name as Maryham and described her lifetime supporting the teachings of a man she referred to as Jesus. A young, dark-skinned blind girl, singing mantras as her only devotion in a life that would have otherwise felt empty and helpless, drifted forward to be recognized. A fairy glistening like water in the sunshine hovered above me, radiating the fairy consciousness. The fairy, named Oraia Naraia, demonstrated that my soul visited other dimensions and planets for study, taking on their form for a lifetime. Each of these characters demonstrated the diverse levels of my soul. I noticed the ratio of female lifetimes was greater than male lifetimes, and the presence of the goddess felt strong within my soul, yet that was not something I had previously related to the Celestial White Beings.

"We, like you and every soul on Earth and the inner planes, hold and allow all that is the Creator to flow through us. Each of us, whether existing as separate beings or united consciousness, can access the complete abundance of the Creator. The Creator is an abundant source of light and energy; its creations, expansion, consciousness, and qualities are limitless. As beings on Earth or the inner planes, we cannot possibly express all that is the Creator; therefore, we connect with and express aspects of the Creator through our beings to aid our journey, our divine purpose, and our self-exploration," the Celestial White Beings gently explained.

The aspects and characters of my soul began to diminish. They had served their purpose in connecting me on a deeper level with my soul. My consciousness and awareness now drifted in the pure white light with hints of the pink, blue, and gold of my soul light. Still, I was aware of my physical body loudly chanting my soul tones in the temple.

"*Om* is the eternal vibration of the universe or the Creator," the Celestial White Beings explained. "*Na* means bliss, which is the ultimate state of realization of the Creator. *Ka* refers to the energy of the Creator and the ultimate energetic form of your being as an instrument of the Creator's light, while *Ta* symbolizes life. *Ma* encapsulates the balanced feminine vibration of the Creator, while *Ra* captures the balanced masculine vibration. The mantra is a powerful intention to place and encourage the divine into the cells of your physical body and all aspects of your being. Nara, although the mantra is connected to your soul and soul group, you can share and teach it to others to aid them in an enhanced connection with their souls and divine selves.

"Each person's soul has a name, sound, symbol, and even colors that can be accessed to aid fuller understanding of the soul. It is not vital to access these expressions of the soul; however, they can be used as tools for further soul exploration. It is beautiful to allow your soul to come forth in creative ways, such as singing, dancing, poetry, drawing, and so forth. We have achieved this with you before, Nara. You might think you have integrated your soul, yet there are many levels of soul integration. Each new level that you access might express itself differently through your being." The wisdom of the Celestial White Beings rang true in my mind.

"Nara, we wish to transport you to the fourteenth dimension where an aspect of our energy resides." The Celestial White Beings spoke with the feeling of a direct and powerful purpose.

The white light of my soul intensified as the Celestial White Beings drew closer into my energetic field. They were quickening the vibration of my being so that I would shift from being conscious of my physical reality and place my conscious awareness into the fourteenth dimension. I knew then that the Celestial White Beings exist in this dimension and beyond. I was aware we had entered a small golden light chamber similar to a cocoon, which was often used for healing. As the Celestial White Beings steadied my vibrational speed to ground me in my new reality, I felt their energy step back, giving me time to adjust to my surroundings. Gradually, the vibrant white light that had been blazing in my vision dissipated until a single white form remained before me. With the Celestial White Beings forming a circle around us, I noticed protruding from my heart center the symbol I had seen on my hand when holding hands with Benjamin. Although the single white form before me held slightly more blue light than my own soul, an almost identical symbol from its heart center reflected at me. There was an intense sense of familiarity and recognition and a powerful pull of connection between us. Both our energies began to spiral from the floor upward through our beings. It was then that I glimpsed through the light Benjamin's physical form exactly as I had seen him at the full moon celebration.

"The energy of the Celestial White Beings has been supporting Earth since its creation. We hold within our consciousness the eternal divine plan given forth by the Creator. We can see the larger picture of the purpose of Earth and the journey all souls and soul groups within the universe are embarking on. We are asked by the Creator to place aspects of ourselves on Earth to play key roles in Earth's journey. Every soul group is guided to do the same.

"Nara, you are an aspect of our soul. You are the physical receiver and distributor of our energies on Earth. In the changing times of Atlantis, you can no longer do this alone. Within your divine plan, it was always written that you would connect with another soul aspect of the Celestial White Beings existing on Earth in a male body. Your existence with this male form of our energies will aid us in understanding the balance between the masculine and feminine aspects of the Creator, the experience of a pure heart connection and a oneness relationship, so that we can use the consciousness discovered as an imprint to aid the spiritual evolution of other civilizations. We are discovering and collecting consciousness from your existence on Earth, Nara, that can be distributed to many across the universe while aiding our understanding of the Creator.

"Benjamin is the stabilizer and protector of our energy, symbolizing that he can choose a dimension for us to exist within by stabilizing our vibration so that you can receive our energies. He is the master of balance, also holding the ability of balancing and protecting your energies, Nara. Benjamin has studied on Venus with the Pleiadians and Arcturians. We placed him on Earth before your birth because we knew the divine plan that would unfold. Of course, your soul aspect recognizes and loves the soul before you whom your personality knows as Benjamin. Your connection is strong because, we remind you, we have sent you both to other stars, planets, and even universes to evolve and understand on our behalf. You are our beacons, our communicators, and our travelers of the universe in search of greater realizations of all that is the Creator. In this time of change on Atlantis, we bring you together to experience love while you discover and assist the heightening of the vibration of Atlantis before it becomes too low to restore. There is much for you to activate and explore within each other to physically interpret and gain understanding of our energies on Earth. Together you will become a powerful beacon of light on Earth to support many."

As I listened intently to the consciousness of the Celestial White Beings, I felt familiarity, recognition, and truth build within my being. I was only able to understand the situation and perceive the soul before me from the perspective of Nara, yet my soul was swelling with bliss. In my temple on Atlantis, I had always known a feeling of loneliness, which often smothered me during long periods of being in the temple by myself. I thought the loneliness came from my physical experience of separation from my home on the inner planes, from the Celestial White Beings, from my guides and friends. Suddenly I saw that my soul and everything I existed as on Earth as Nara simply wished to share my spiritual experiences with another who would fully comprehend me. I thought Jayda was the one whom I would share my soul with, merging my light and consciousness with his to experience the Creator more fully. Finally, I understood that Jayda might have prepared me for experiencing unification with my soul mate, a being from the same soul group as I and with whom I could physically, energetically, and consciously share my light with. With this realization, the heaviness that had frequently rested in my heart lifted, and my soul streamed forward to Benjamin like ribbons of light connecting into his energy. Memories of our experiences together flooded back into my awareness. Creations of love, bliss, truth, joy, and peace exploded as our energies intertwined, reacquainting us once more. Our connection formed a beautiful painting of light between us, presenting itself as a map of knowingness for us to explore.

"Nara, I step forward to support, protect, and honor you. I am Benjamin, also known as OmSe Na. There is much for us to achieve together on Earth. Our purpose is to be white beacons on Earth to aid the survival of Atlantis; we are the White Beacons of Atlantis." Benjamin's words pulsated throughout my entire being as if they were my own. His energy felt like it was lifting me further into the light of the Creator, empowering me to see the truth of my being and purpose on Earth.

"The Celestial White Beings have shared much information with me concerning the future of Atlantis, and as your protector, I cannot share it all — although I am permitted to share some information." I gently signalled for Benjamin to continue, giving my consent that I was ready to accept his insights.

"Nara, within you, there is a seed of creation that was also planted in the earth by the Celestial White Beings during the creation of the planet. You carry the energy vibration within your soul identical to that planted into the earth. Not only is the vibration an imprint of the Creator's divine plan, but it is also the consciousness of the Celestial White Beings — their profound wisdom and awareness of the universe and the Creator. It is the healing template of the Celestial White Beings, which if revealed to Earth and humanity in its entirety, would create a mass healing and ascension to higher dimensions. Such vibrations and imprints have been gradually placed within your soul since your birth.

"As your soul steps forward to be in action within your physical body, these vibrations and imprints enter your physical body to be transmitted across Atlantis. Nara, you hold the energy that can remind those on Earth of returning to the oneness and love of the Creator so that peace can prevail. I am here to protect you and to support you in the mission unfolding before you."

Benjamin's message of dedication and love was filled with an honesty that was awe inspiring and irresistible. Every part of my being absorbed his words as feelings of knowingness, remembrance, and awareness of the seed of creation grew within me. In all their conversations with me, the Celestial White Beings had never mentioned the seed of creation, and I wondered why they had kept such important information from me. Yet it felt appropriate for Benjamin to deliver this wisdom. He continued.

"As Atlantis and the Atlanteans began to thrive and to build the civilization we recognize today, the original attraction to the discovery of spiritual connection and scientific experiment was balanced and explored equally with an open perspective. Gradually, some groups began to favor a pathway of spiritual connection with the Creator as a way of life while others favored the scientific approach to daily life. The latter encouraged a lessening of the soul in action within the physical body, mind, and personality, reducing the power of the Creator within their beings. Thus their bodies and chakras became undernourished from lack of light and love while their minds and mental bodies expanded to become the overriding influence. If the soul isn't in action to a high degree within the being, then the mind draws on the ego, past experiences, beliefs, and influences from others as fuel for understanding and creation. If imbalance and disconnection from the Creator are experienced within, then the same is projected outward to each person's reality. The magic, creative flow, and divine synchronicity vanish as the mind begins to create the physical reality, which can often result in dissatisfaction, limitations, and suffering.

"The ego is becoming more powerful within the minds of many. The ego states that it, or you as a physical being, knows better than the Creator. The purpose of life on Earth is to surrender to the divine flow of the Creator, using this constant surge of energy within your being to create and manifest. Once you hinder the divine flow of the Creator, you can become stagnant and limited. This encourages the mind to develop tools outward of itself in the physical reality, such as machines and technology, to replace and compensate for the restrictions experienced within. On Atlantis, those who are focused on scientific development are growing in power and strength, and they might risk the energetic and magnetic balance of Earth's structure to advance their technology."

I interrupted Benjamin's flow. "What can we do to resolve this situation?" My heart and soul wanted to be of service in any way that would support Atlantis.

"It is our purpose to bring forth a deep remembrance of the freedom and truth within the experience of a connection with the Creator to those who have forgotten. This is all I can share with you at this time. Please know I am here to support and love you, offering to you the protection of the Celestial White Beings, Nara." Benjamin's consciousness flowed gently into my own as if I were experiencing the most beautiful embrace.

I drifted in the energy and consciousness for some time, enjoying the shifts the light created as it penetrated my being. I felt at home surrounded by my soul group, the Celestial White Beings. With time, I realized my body ached from sitting on the hard, cold floor of my temple, and I was aware of the stillness surrounding me as my automatic chanting came to a cycle of completion.

Nara's Notes

Sound is an important aspect of spiritual growth because high-vibrational sounds — such as the frequency of a singing bowl, uplifting music, chanting sacred words, or toning the word *"Om"* — penetrate the body and auric field, encouraging the cells to vibrate at the same frequency as the sound. Your entire body begins to vibrate in harmony, and it is from this state of being and awareness that you become more able to absorb and accept the higher frequency of the Creator. When there is pain, suffering, or disharmony of any kind within the body, mind, emotions, or auric field, sound can be used to create harmony and peace, therefore welcoming a solution or healing into your situation. Sound can also be used to create sacred spaces or to quickly attune yourself to the peace, love, and bliss of the Creator.

Practice 8
Mind Mastery

I encourage you to practice chanting the mantra *"Om, Na, Ka, Ta, Ma, Ra"* out loud for five minutes with your eyes closed. Gradually lengthen the time you spend focused on the mantra. While chanting, it is important to allow the focus of your mind to be present with the mantra. Each time a thought enters your mind and awareness that causes you to become distracted from the mantra, bring your attention back to it.

You might find it beneficial to say the mantra, inhale, exhale, and begin again. Imagine the mantra is someone you love deeply; you wish to be present with and aware of all their actions constantly. In this way, you become aware of the influence of the mantra on your being and mind. You become intimate with its vibration and presence within your mind as it filters to bring harmony within your entire being.

Practice 9
Soul Sounding

Every soul on Earth within a physical body is sacred, special, and deeply loved. You are included in this statement. Like everyone else, you have seeds of light, sacred imprints, codes, and vibrations, along with consciousness and wisdom, that have been placed into your soul since your birth. As your soul comes into action within your physical body and reality on Earth, these sacred vibrations and imprints from your soul group merge with your entire being. As I discovered from the Celestial White Beings, my soul holds a vibration that can heal and return humanity's focus to the vibration of oneness and unity with the Creator. You also have a sacred energy that is almost akin to a light elixir within your, and it has a purpose of supporting the ascension of humanity when you radiate and express your soul light.

You can often identify the purpose of your soul light by exploring how the quality of your soul energy feels like to you. You might sense it as love, serenity, strength, or any other sacred quality. With an understanding of the quality or qualities held within your soul, you are more able to understand the purpose of your soul — how it supports you and others — as you imagine its light radiating from within your being and extending into your surroundings and beyond limitations.

Imagine a ball of light or a flame at your heart chakra. Let the light expand with each breath you exhale. When you feel in profound connection and observation of your soul, ask to be made aware of the quality or qualities your soul emanates connected to its purpose on Earth. Sit in patient meditation and observation of any thoughts, feelings, or sensations that may arise.

You might then want to tone the syllable *"Om,"* the eternal sound of the universe of the Creator. Open your mouth to begin with the *O* sound, and as you enter into the *M* sound, allow your mouth to close as the sound continues — until your breath runs out. Inhale deeply, and begin to sound on your exhale. Focus on your soul as you experience the sound: Each time you exhale the sound, you expand your soul and bring it forth for further expression.

You will notice the sound begins to alter. It might feel like you are being creative, and the tone of *"Om"* might disappear, altering into a personal sound that will be an expression of your soul, or your soul sound. Soul sounding encourages the vibration of your soul to be in action, pulsating within your entire being.

Explore this practice, giving yourself the time to allow the creativity of your soul to emerge. You might notice the sound of your soul constantly alters, or it might remain the same. It is your unique and personal sound; there are no rules or limitations. The sound creates a bridge between the energetic inner-planes reality and the physical reality.

5

Grandfather Hamna

Hamna rose to his feet to envelop me in a warm embrace. "Beloved Nara, I have been expecting you. My mind has been filled with thoughts of you for some time."

I had stumbled across Hamna sitting beneath a tree while I walked in the countryside to support the grounding of my soul. I was consciously aware of the contact of my feet with the earth to encourage my soul and the divine flow of the Creator to move into my earth star chakra below my feet, becoming more fully manifest within my being and physical reality.

"How did you know I would be here?" I replied with surprise.

Hamna smiled, his eyes twinkling. It was, of course, his intuition and inner knowingness that had guided him to the most appropriate place to meet and connect with me. Hamna gestured for me to sit down with him beneath the tree's canopy.

Hamna was not only my grandfather. He was also a wise Melchizedek disciple and appointed by the Celestial White Beings as a guardian of my temple. He was married to Violet. They had been promised to each other from birth, as the priestesses at their births noticed (although they were born five years apart) a destiny and connection between them. They had a purpose on Earth together, so the priestesses granted permission for them to marry when they became of age in the central temples, their place of study.

Hamna looked more like Parlo's older brother than his father; they both had light brown hair and dark brown eyes. Hamna was much calmer and more centered than Parlo, choosing to frequently sit in meditation for days to maintain his mastery and discipline while being most at home within nature.

To me, Hamna always seemed like the leader of our community. This had more to do with his strong inner wisdom than his leadership skills. Sitting down with Hamna, I opened my heart, accepting my trust and faith in his knowledge and wisdom. Hamna had always taught me to remain in my power, even when he spoke teachings from the sacred realms of the inner planes, signifying I was to observe his wisdom and accept only what resonated with my being.

"You have been having some beautiful experiences of integration with your soul and soul group, Nara." Hamna paused to receive my confirmation. "However, you require additional information to aid complete understanding at the physical and personality levels." Again I nodded and waited for him to continue.

"You have been aware of your soul group, the Celestial White Beings, from such a young age, and now you are entering a period when you will work as one with them to aid Atlantis. The way masters and teachers share their spiritual wisdom on Earth no longer captivates many in our civilization. New insight and perspective are required, as well as a healing vibration so powerful that it will jolt many into remembrance of the divine within them. The vibration of Atlantis is lowering as more people become preoccupied with technology and material aspects of life rather than the presence of the Creator within them — friendship, love, inner truth, peace, happiness, and an existence beyond suffering. With the mind's preoccupation with technological advances comes separation from the soul and its divine intuition.

"Nara, for some time now, I have not been returning energetically through meditation and energetic projection to the Melchizedek Temple that was once my home. Each time I connected with the temple, which in the past held such a sweet vibration of love, I encountered dark, fearful thoughts. Many Melchizedek disciples have succumbed to fear and no longer hold faith in the Creator. I have been guided to sever all cords of attachment to the temple to safeguard my energy and our reality here in north Atlantis. My actions unsettle me, as they bring my awareness to the reality of Atlantis falling from its high vibrations more quickly than we expected. Do you remember how fear is created, Nara?" Hamna paused to gaze at me.

This was a question Hamna had often asked me as a child, so it felt deliciously familiar to me. "Fear is created when a person allows a negative thought to enter his or her mind-space. If the person chooses to focus on the negative thought, collecting and carrying it on the journey of life, the thought becomes a belief. Many of our beliefs are projected into our reality, so any negative beliefs we hold can be manifested within our physical reality for our experience. If the belief is negative or misaligned with the Creator, the experience is most likely undesirable, so fear builds within the emotional body as a powerful fuel for the belief. When fear arises, it is actually a feeling of being separate from the Creator — helpless, powerless, and unloved. The person accepts these feelings and distances him- or herself from the Creator, ignoring the divine aspect of the Creator within his or her being, which causes further experiences of suffering and pain. This can continue in multiple cycles, which can be difficult to break and could create more beliefs of a similar nature. Reality begins to offer confirmation that the fears are relevant, which signifies the beliefs and fears are embedded at a cellular level. Shifting back into a space and focusing on love is the only method to promote healing and restore balance."

Hamna smiled at my explanation, knowing it was something he had shared with me long ago. "Many priests and priestesses understand the development of fear. However, knowledge can sometimes be difficult to integrate into reality; it doesn't always signify embodiment. I believe the advancement of technology has encouraged many to look outside of themselves for tools and assistance, which has caused a perspective of separation, allowing negative and unproductive thoughts to pollute the mind. A cycle can begin without a person's noticing. The ego then gains power, taking control and influencing the projections of the mind into the physical reality. I believe this is occurring within the central temples of Atlantis, and I sense that it is spreading into other areas of Atlantis."

"So love is our greatest tool and defense," I affirmed.

"Nara, you and your Celestial White Beings are also our security, protection, and answer — as well as Benjamin." Haman's eyes penetrated mine. "I am aware of many divine plans unfolding now," he confirmed. "We will all be asked to play a role in the circumstances, challenges, and that divine plan." This was always Hamna's way to point out how special I was and then to remind me I was equal to all, maintaining the state of humbleness within my being.

"Why Benjamin, though? Hamna, he is a stranger to me."

Hamna laughed at my personality's unwillingness to accept Benjamin. I remembered my meeting with the Celestial White Beings and Benjamin; however, back in the harsh energies of solid reality, it felt like a dream or a hallucination.

"It is true that as the personality, you know very little of Benjamin. You have hardly spoken to each other, yet the Creator is weaving a divine plan, bringing you together. The Celestial White Beings have agreed to this divine plan and support numerous synchronicities within your reality. Your connection with Benjamin is vital now, as when you both unite your energies through acceptance of each other at this earthly level, many divine pathways will fall into place. All the knowledge you have collected — memories and connections with the inner planes of the Creator's universe — will fall into alignment with your energies, flowing through both of you with a powerful force that can be wielded to support Atlantis. You are instruments for divine wisdom and templates from the Creator that are being transmitted through the Celestial White Beings to anchor into the earth. This doesn't signify that you are special; you have simply been chosen to play a divine role in the reality unfolding before us."

Hamna's eyes scanned me, examining whether I was letting go of my unwillingness to accept Benjamin.

"I still don't understand why we have been chosen," I confessed, feeling somewhat frustrated with myself. I didn't want to disappoint Hamna.

"You have been chosen because you are from the same soul group. You are one and have the same energy so that you can work together in tremendous peace and harmony. You have achieved similar transmissions of light from the Creator through the Celestial White Beings in many other realities, lifetimes, and civilizations.

"Because your souls have unity, you represent the masculine and feminine aspect of the Creator. By working in oneness and love, you can anchor a vibration of harmony into Earth's energetic template to bring balance to the masculine and feminine vibrations of the Creator — the God and Goddess. When both aspects of the Creator are integrated, when there is no identification of masculine and feminine vibrations but simply a divine purity, the highest unity and vibration of the Creator can be experienced."

Hamna paused to confirm that I understood his words. I felt lighter and brighter in my energy as Hamna's explanation created a shift in my body, encouraging me to be open and accepting of the situation unfolding in my reality. Content with my progress, he continued.

"Remember, you do not need a connection with another person to bring balance and harmony to your own masculine and feminine; however, the Creator is choosing to demonstrate integration through your and Benjamin's presence on Earth at this time. It is important for both of you to follow the divine intuition of your souls, as this will be the Creator speaking the divine plan to you for all that needs to take place to manifest. The divine plan of the Creator might not be what you as a personality would desire to manifest, so trust in and attention to your intuition is essential at this time." Hamna paused for a moment as if to emphasize his next words: "Nara, you will discover all you seek with Benjamin because he acts as a mirror for you to delve deeper into your understanding of yourself. Maybe your resistance to accepting Benjamin, your that he is a stranger, is your unwillingness to accept or see yourself with greater comprehension."

"Hamna, what is a soul mate?" I asked gingerly, still trying to comprehend my connection with Benjamin.

"We are all soul mates to each other. We accompany each other on a journey home to unity and oneness with the Creator. 'Soul mate' is a label often signifying souls from the same soul group who connect and realize the same within each other. In truth, you do not have to be from the same soul group to experience a true soul connection with another person. Connections are feelings of remembrance. Often you travel through multiple lifetimes with the same souls. These souls might be from different soul groups than yours, yet there is a strong bond of familiarity between you, which could be explained as soul mates — strong soul friendships.

"We each extend from a soul group, and the soul group is an extension of the Creator. Your soul group is focused on returning to unity with the Creator. Soul groups frequently work together, which activates feelings of familiarity within your being. In truth, you are aware of and as one with all aspects of the Creator. Each is a family member, so you could say they are all soul mates for you." This was information I needed to hear. Remembering my connection with each person entering my life was valuable in my quest to experience the Creator fully.

"Nara, you have a strong connection with the community that has formed around you now in Atlantis. You have lived many lifetimes with these souls. In a period named Lemuria, which began before Atlantis, you and Benjamin incarnated with many present within our community. Lemurians had etheric bodies and achieved great spiritual advancements that were especially focused on realization of the soul. They used a small amount of technology but found it difficult to sustain their high vibration at an earthly level because food was lacking and the soul couldn't cope with the heavy energies of the physical level; often, they would die in midadulthood. You existed alongside Benjamin in that lifetime so that you could learn through reflection of your truth. You were named Nadia, meaning beginning, and Benjamin was named Celestyn, meaning a being from heaven. The high vibration you experienced in Lemuria is something you wish to bring to your current lifetime in Atlantis."

I gasped in wonder. Everything Hamna was sharing resonated with me deeply. His tone was informative yet lovingly supportive, and energy flowed to me as if parts of myself and my consciousness were returning to me. I was excited to hear more, so I encouraged him to recommence.

"As the civilization of Atlantis emerged, more souls from the universe of the Creator incarnated on Earth. Our civilization was prosperous and abundant in food, creating healthy physical bodies, and souls were also beginning to understand the process of existing within the physical and material levels of energy. Thus the life expectancy of Atlanteans increased, and the volume of souls incarnate on Earth rose. After your first lifetime on Earth during the time of Lemuria, you returned to the inner planes to visit the Universal School of Light, which further prepared you for your existence within a denser physical vibration while allowing you to set the date and other details for your return to Earth.

"This time when you entered Atlantis, your soul group chose to place you and Benjamin on opposite sides of the Atlantean plane. Named Cara, meaning beloved, and Benesh, meaning blessed, your separation instigated an experience of loneliness that accelerated your spiritual evolvement and self-awareness."

Hamna smiled at me with a gentle compassion and knowingness. I knew he was aware of the loneliness I had experienced in my current lifetime as well as my secret longing for a beloved one to share my life with. I had long ago given up trying to hide anything from Hamna, but even so, I felt slightly awkward, as if my deepest desires and feelings were visible. He gently placed his hand on my lower back to comfort me.

"Nara, you then returned to Atlantis to study in the crystalline temples of Isis and develop yourself as a priestess. Benjamin was present in that lifetime; however, your connection and a blessing of your relationship were denied by the priestesses, causing much anguish. Now in the third civilization of Atlantis, you have returned as Benjamin and Nara, living separately first to instigate a powerful spiritual growth so that when you unite, you will merge to become powerful beacons of light.

"Nara, your personal purpose is to evolve your creative, loving, and nourishing qualities, and to express these, there is a need for you to be in your own power. Thus you will be able to discover your masculine qualities more fully. Benjamin holds a purpose of reintroducing feminine qualities through the opening of his heart chakra."

Hamna fell silent, observing me as I processed his information.

"So Benjamin and I really do know each other, and this lifetime isn't a new journey together; it is a continuation of something begun long ago." I felt all my confusion dissolve as I finally accepted the divine will of the Creator, the Celestial White Beings, and my soul.

Hamna simply smiled with knowingness. I had received the information I needed through him at this time.

"Hamna, maybe it is not my place to question you, as I know I must draw wisdom and answers from my divine inner guidance, but what are Benjamin and I to do together? How are we to support Atlantis and our people in accelerating our vibrations?" Suddenly I felt lost, realizing I had no understanding of my purpose in supporting Atlantis.

Hamna smiled sympathetically. He not only understood the divine plan of the Creator for my reality but also recognized the overwhelming feeling of the unknown that seemed like a burden on my shoulders.

"With the development of your connection to Benjamin, you will discover that you enhance each other's energy, allowing guidance to flow forth as you accept of each other. There is no need for your concern. Everything is flowing and will continue to flow with the perfection of the Creator."

Hamna rose to his feet and began to follow the pathway back to the village. He didn't need to say goodbye, because he knew we would connect soon at a physical level and were always connected energetically. He was confident he had shared all the Creator wished him to express and was content in his own role in the divine plan unfolding for Atlantis.

Nara's Notes

A divine plan is a scenario, situation, or experience guided by the Creator. It is created through the cocreation of your soul, soul group, guides, and the Creator, often encapsulating lessons your soul wishes to master and learn. A divine plan is akin to a larger picture of your reality; it doesn't only focus on your present moment but is a plan for your entire lifetime, which is synchronized with the divine plans of every other soul on Earth and the inner planes, creating a divine plan for Earth and the universe of the Creator. Within a personal divine plan or a divine plan for humanity, the abundant flow of the Creator is present, allowing everything to evolve with perfection, truth, and ease. It is akin to a structure or a map you cannot escape — even though you have free will on Earth. Your free will offers you the option to follow your inner guidance, to be happy, and to allow your life experiences to flow with ease, encouraging great life lessons to be overcome effortlessly.

If you choose not to follow your inner guidance, you might discover that your life becomes difficult and maybe even painful. This is not because the Creator wishes to punish you; it is because you are battling the divine flow of the Creator, which is like trying to walk through a tidal wave. Even with a divine plan in place, you have freedom of expression, action, and reaction, which influence your life tremendously. Often the painful experiences in your reality are not a part of your divine plan; they are creations from the belief systems and perspectives of your mind. In the time of Atlantis, the divine plan was very strong, which meant our lives were planned by our souls before our birth and usually didn't alter or shift much throughout our entire lifetimes.

In your time of ascension, your divine plan is constantly developing and rewritten by your soul in every given moment. Your free will is far more influential in your reality, and you have the ability to create and manifest from the guidance within. This means you are in control and hold responsibility in your reality and in the spiritual advancement of your soul, which, when you are on the Earth plane, you cannot truly gain a clear understanding of due to the density of the energy. With every soul's divine plan in constant evolution, this signifies that the divine plan of the universe constantly shifts, yet there is always a continued unified and complete goal or destination. Every soul naturally works, processes, and exists as one, so this becomes present in the divine plan for all. Even though you have such freedom, landmarks are still mapped out for you by your soul, and you are guided to experience them.

You might never truly grasp or understand your divine plan in this lifetime. However, it is important to accept the energy vibration of your divine plan from the Creator through your soul group and soul, emanating it throughout your entire being. Acceptance is feeling comfortable with the energy that enters your reality and welcoming it with understanding; you can accept energies or situations that frustrate you or cause pain. Acceptance does not mean tolerance, but more so realizing that something has been created either by the Creator or you for a divine reason. With acceptance, you allow recognition of the energy or situation in your reality, and then, from a place of love, you are able to let it go — to heal and release it. It is often with acceptance that you can shield yourself from pain or suffering because you acknowledge its creation and existence within your reality with a neutral or loving reaction, which means its impact on your reality is lessened. Accepting the energy of your divine plan while also practicing acceptance or responsibility for the manifestations within your reality are key to allowing yourself to move in rhythm with the divine flow of the Creator. Remember, acceptance is acknowledgment, responsibility, recognition, and appreciation.

Practice 10
Accept Your Divine Plan

Focusing on your breathing, allow yourself to enter a state of peace and contentment. When you are ready, say out loud,

I am now ready to accept the energetic vibration of the divine plan cocreated by the Creator, my soul group, and my soul for my present reality. I open myself up to experience the divine plan of the Creator flowing through me with great ease. If I am to understand divine guidance to aid my current reality, I permit this to flow into my conscious awareness now. Thank you.

Take the attention of your mind to your heart chakra and imagine, sense, or acknowledge the most precious book existing within your heart chakra. This book contains your divine plan for your current reality.

Imagine, sense, or acknowledge a pristine beam of golden light flowing through your crown chakra at the top of your head into your heart center and this book as you allow yourself to accept the divine plan of the Creator.

Inhale. Allow the golden light to flow into your crown chakra. Exhale. Let it fill your heart center.

You may recognize the book as it opens. You may be able to read wisdom on the pages and gain a feeling, inspirational sensation, or words or visions that act as messages of guidance from your divine plan, which is the cocreation and guidance of the Creator, your soul group, and your soul. Even if you do not receive any form of guidance, you are still absorbing the energies. They are becoming more active within your reality and will emerge with divine timing.

Finish by breathing the golden light into your body, your surroundings, and the earth.

Practice 11
Be in the Divine Flow

Existing in the divine flow of the Creator means you are constantly supported, guided, and assisted in your reality. There is not a moment when you are alone or helpless; everything is always provided for you. There is simply a need to recognize this and know you are worthy to receive.

The most challenging aspect of being in the flow of the Creator is remaining in a state in which you are conscious of the Creator and the Creator's energy flowing through you into your reality as you also grasp the guidance rising from within your being. I wish to share with you a three-part process to support your understanding and advancement in this area.

PART 1
First, focus on your breathing, gaining a state of meditation. Then say out loud,

I now permit myself to consciously exist in the divine flow of the Creator.

Imagine, sense, or acknowledge a downpour of energy — like a spotlight flowing over and through your being — from the central energy of the Creator.

Observe the colors of the light and any feelings, sensations, or ideas as you simply allow energy to flow almost like electricity through and from your being.

Focus on this until you begin to feel, sense, or acknowledge the presence of the flow of energy.

PART 2

With the flow of energy circulating through and over your being while also emanating in all directions, ask the divine flow of the Creator to guide and influence movement in your body. (You may wish to stand up to experience this.) Allow your guidance or inspiration to rise from within you and influence movement within your body. They might be small movements or big rhythmic movements. Do not force the process, but rather listen to the energy and how it wishes to influence your physical body.

With this process, you can have a lot of fun. You also allow yourself to determine and recognize your inner guidance. It may instantly influence your body, encouraging you to feel its flow and impact; or it may guide you with words or an insight, encouraging you to move a certain part of your body.

Practice this. You might want to play some music to support your expression. You are building a relationship and a realization of your intuition and inner guidance, which is always present but often ignored or disregarded. Remember, the divine flow of the Creator is your soul, soul group, and the Creator; it is you consciously existing in their spotlight, moving as one with their energy — which, of course, is your energy.

PART 3

Throughout your day, bring the attention of your mind back to a remembrance and recognition that you exist in the divine flow of the Creator.

Second, whenever you need to make a decision, let yourself first remember you are connected into and exist as the divine flow of the Creator. Then ask for guidance, support, or assistance to enter your awareness to aid you in being inspired by the flow of the Creator.

This can be as simple as asking what food will serve you for your breakfast or what color of clothing will serve you for the day ahead. It is developing the understanding that all answers are available to you because you exist in the divine flow of the Creator. In many ways, there is no need for you to think; simply accept inspiration from the Creator.

CHAPTER

6

Forming Divine Relationships

I arrived at the temple early for the transmission of the Celestial White Beings'
energy and consciousness to the people of our community. Each week, those of
the community who felt guided to gathered within the temple to gain support
from the Celestial White Beings. It was a space for us to connect with each other,
to advance our spiritual ascension through the group vibration and consciousness as well as to encourage the strengthening of our community energy. The
Celestial White Beings instigated this from the very beginning of the manifestation of my temple with the purpose of promoting oneness within our community. If the community surrounding the temple held a high vibration and a
powerful group consciousness of unity, then this would support and maintain
the high vibrations of the temple as if the community were the foundation of the
temple. To me, this made perfect sense; if chaos surrounded the temple, it would
hinder its radiance.

To my surprise, many people were already gathered within the temple, sitting
cross-legged with their backs against the temple wall. The temple was filled with
a pure white mist that danced around the people present. The Celestial White
Beings were already there communing with the souls of the people. I walked to
my cushion, which had been placed within the center of the space, and made
myself comfortable and ready for the transmission. More and more people
entered the temple, quickly finding a space and then acknowledging and greeting the Celestial White Beings in their own special ways. It was difficult to make
out the faces of those gathered as the mist that was the presence of the Celestial
White Beings intensified.

"Beloved Celestial White Beings, I love you with every cell of my body and every vibration of my soul." With my hands at my heart chakra, I spoke my words mentally, exuding gratitude and love. "I recognize our oneness and unity and the presence of our united love within me. I am here to be your instrument and to bring forth all that is needed to be of service to all aspects of the Creator present on Earth and within the Creator's universe. I open myself up to work as one with you now."

The energy of the Celestial White Beings instantly entered my being through my crown chakra, creating what can only be described as a crystal pillar of magnificent light within my torso. The crystal seemed to generate an enormous amount of white light, pumping it through every part of my being and into my surroundings. The energy was strong, almost as if it were solid, as it reached out from my being into the hearts and entire chakra systems of each person present, creating the same crystal-like pillar of magnificent light within their beings. I felt the energy jolt and jump slightly as people shifted old, unneeded energies to enter complete alignment with the energy of the light, holding a similar energetic vibration. To me, we felt like a sturdy wheel of light; I was at the center with the Celestial White Beings acting as the spokes holding us all as one. With the group's energy vibration continuing to quicken, I didn't notice we were drifting from the temple into other dimensions and levels of energy beyond Earth.

"We are transporting you all to the angelic kingdom." I heard these words come out of my mouth.

Our bodies were still in the temple, yet our combined consciousness was shifting into the dimensions of the angelic kingdom. Beautiful pink and blue lights merged and melted into the pure white light we were experiencing. Impressions of divine beauty, grace, peace, and tender love filled our senses as angels joined us.

"We now exist in the angelic chamber of divine relationships." Again, my voice carried the words of the Celestial White Beings forward.

Into my vision came the most beautiful angelic being. In many ways, it was formless, yet it was tall and all encompassing, and it exuded elegance and grace with a balanced male and female vibration. Warmth hit my senses as the unconditional and selfless love the angel emanated embraced me completely. Feelings of joy, bliss, and surrender to freedom filled my being. My soul was soaring high as I experienced the simple embrace of an angelic being. I felt as if I were touching the Creator, touching truth, and experiencing the purity of love.

"You are each being embraced by an angelic being. You do not need to understand this being; simply accept the experience. When you experience the embrace of an angelic being, you truly know how divine connections and relationships can feel. Know the angel is embracing you with its energy. Notice the angel is connecting with your soul, recognizing your truth, respecting your presence, and existing in complete joy and gratitude to be one with you while remaining within its own energy and power.

"If you can allow yourself to accept an embrace and divine connection with an angelic being, then you will notice how you react — whether you feel worthy or uncomfortable. Be aware of how your entire being responds to the embrace, and allow yourself to mirror the embrace of the angelic being. Not through thought or imagination but through acceptance, you can offer a similar embrace of the same influence to the angelic being. Let your entire being open up, let go of limitations, and allow your energy and love to flow freely. It is probably true that if you were to imagine you were embracing an angelic being, then you would embrace and connect with its energy in a different way from embracing a person on Earth, whether that person is a stranger or a loved one. We sense you can feel the healing that is taking place through this union, the openness of your energy and soul. This is a true connection free from any outside influences. Your souls are communing with the angelic beings without limitations and boundaries.

"It is not so much the embrace that is important but the openness and acceptance of each other. You can experience the same thing with any and every being and soul on Earth or the inner planes — even without an embrace. A divine relationship is your openness, your willingness to accept and to radiate from a place of constant peace and love within your being, free from fear. Relationships are not about likes or dislikes; they are about the connection of the soul and the willingness to allow the truth of the Creator to unfold, the willingness to love all beings and be loved by the Creator. Can you imagine the world if everyone connected with each other with this perspective? Of course, how you express your connection with loved ones would be different from your actions with strangers, but the energetic understanding, respect, and acceptance would remain the same with all beings."
The words of the Celestial White Beings hung in my mind and the air.

We remained suspended in this state of communion with the angelic vibration for some time. Gradually, as our experience came to completion, we found ourselves drifting back to being conscious and aware of the temple once more. The Celestial White Beings' energy slowly withdrew from the temple, leaving us to fully enter back into our physical bodies and realities. A stirring in the temple encouraged me to bring my attention from beautiful states of bliss, like waves washing over and through me, to open my eyes and observe those around me. With remembrance in their hearts of their recent experience, people rose from their sitting positions to hug each other. I watched them linger in each other's arms to allow their souls' energy to commune with the intention of acceptance and radiance of each other. The room was beginning to buzz with love; I could feel it in the atmosphere, exuding from everyone's bodies and eyes. A deeper exchange of love occurred than I had previously experienced. I know that the Celestial White Beings had shared a priceless gift with us, as the energy we recognized within our beings and within each other filtered into and inspired our entire community, creating a tremendous sense of unity.

"I am going to recognize this energy within my being eternally, sharing it as a radiant beam of light with each person I connect with," I heard one person say to another.

I felt a hand gently rest upon the back of my heart chakra, and somehow it didn't startle me. I looked up, and my eyes met Benjamin's. Reaching down, he scooped me to my feet and wrapped me in his warm embrace. The light exuding from our souls intensified, pulsating with power throughout our bodies. There was a moment when our energies became so activated that I felt as if we were merging. Our souls reached out to each other, existing as one, and I felt as if I was falling deeply into light while being strongly supported from within (and, of course by Benjamin's muscular arms). In the moment of our merging, a profound peace and stillness dawned on me as if there were nothing else — only this moment — as we expanded into each other's light. I can only liken the experience to connecting to and channeling the vibration of the Celestial White Beings.

As my senses gradually connected to the physical plane, I became aware of people leaving the temple. I could see through the open door that it was dusk outside. Gently freeing myself from Benjamin's embrace, I stepped back to take a breath and ground myself back into my reality. Many people grabbed hold of my hand, squeezing it tightly as they filtered past with expressions of gratitude and knowingness of the lessons and consciousness the Celestial White Beings had shared with them. There was an immense sense of contentment and freedom. Glancing around the temple, I saw that only Benjamin remained, standing directly before me with an expression of blissful love. Awkwardness grew between us, as neither of us knew how to react. We had experienced something so profound that words no longer felt relevant or sufficient. Benjamin leaned forward and gently grasped my hand, tugging me gently as he led me from the temple.

"I want to take you to my favorite place in Atlantis," he said as he closed the temple door behind me.

My entire being felt like I was floating on light. I could only follow him because it felt like a tidal wave was rushing us forward. Benjamin were a blue tunic over his sun-kissed skin, his shoulder-length brown hair tied neatly at the nape of his neck. He broke into a gentle run as he led me down the hill into the nature land before the temple. Normally there is a designated pathway that everyone follows to avoid spoiling and disturbing the nature land; however, Benjamin was weaving us through the trees along a new pathway only he knew.

We halted suddenly as we entered a clearing where long grass rippled in the gentle breeze. The stars above us seemed to shine light on one old, large tree standing proudly in the center of the clearing. Lifting his knees up high, Benjamin began to wade through the grass in the direction of the tree. I followed him with a slight sense of bewilderment. Entering the auric field of energy extending from the tree, Benjamin hesitated for a moment before continuing. I knew he was asking permission to enter the tree's space, as was a custom of respect within our community. We stopped together under the low-hanging branches of the tree. Gently releasing my hand, he placed his hands on the trunk of the tree. With a combination of the sight of my third eye and my physical vision, I saw a strong spark of white light flow down the center column of the trunk. White light began to flow simultaneously up and down the trunk, creating a network of light transmitting into the branches and leaves of the tree. Suddenly the whole tree turned white, glistening with shimmering active light. I gasped in amazement and stepped backward. Benjamin gently grasped my left hand and placed it on the tree's trunk.

"The Celestial White Beings!" I gasped, recognizing their energy instantly. "But how can this be?" I looked at him for answers.

"Everything on Atlantis is ready to merge with the Creator, Nara. As you know, it has not been long since my arrival in your community. I was guided to this tree by the Celestial White Beings, whom I recognized as my guides and higher self before I met you and Amka, who reconnected me to a greater understanding of their energy.

"The tree spoke to me. I could hear its words in my mind. It spoke of unity, of wishing to be of greater service, and of a desire to transmit a greater volume of light. I recognized the light of the tree was very active in its physical form; its spirit was moving beyond separation, filtering into its surroundings with the purpose of activating more light within everything its energy connected with. I have seen trees that have well-established spirits or energetic core essences within their physical manifestation; however, this tree was consciously reaching out to support and nurture its surroundings.

"In the presence of the tree, I encouraged the light of the Celestial White Beings to flow through my crown chakra, down my central column, and into the earth, radiating in all directions. The tree mirrored me, achieving the same and connecting to a very pure vibration of the Celestial White Beings. With their energy flowing through the tree, they asked the tree to become a temple for their energy — almost akin to a portal. I feel the Celestial White Beings wish to work with the energy of the trees in the future. I believe they have an idea that the trees of Atlantis will assist in raising the energy vibration of all. I am not sure how this union will manifest; I feel there is a strong purpose building." Benjamin fell silent, momentarily lost in the wonder, excitement, and possibilities that could unfold from this beautiful union of the tree and the Celestial White Beings.

"Does the tree have a name?" I inquired.

"A name?" Benjamin shifted back into our reality.

"Yes. All trees, especially in this area, have names. It is akin to a soul name. It is a name often created from the sound vibration of the tree's essence."

"Um ... I have never heard of that before." Benjamin was intrigued.

I simply closed my eyes and asked the tree directly if it would share its name with us so that we could interpret its energy and connect more fully with it.

"Jacoree," I whispered.

"That's beautiful, Nara." Benjamin sighed. "This is my favorite place in all of Atlantis, and I wanted to share it with you. Will you sit down with me?" He gestured, flattening the grass beside him as he allowed the tree trunk to support his back.

I was happy to join him. His presence now felt so familiar to me that all my previous hesitation melted away. He reached his strong arm around me, drawing me into the warmth of his body. We sat side by side, and I leaned my head on his shoulder.

We sat in silence, sensing each other's presence and allowing knots and blockages in our auras to dissolve and our united presence to strengthen. It felt extremely healing; my heart felt expansive and pulsated with love. I realized I had been waiting for this connection with Benjamin all my life. I had tried to create something similar with Jayda, and while the same experience can occur with two souls from different soul groups, I was now accepting that it was my destiny to work, connect, and communicate with Benjamin on many levels of our beings for the growth of our souls and our soul group and to aid Atlantis. My acceptance of Benjamin seemed to intensify the profound union occurring within us.

"I know it's strange how we have met, and I am aware you were uncertain of me," he said. "I have felt as if I've been searching for someone all my life, and my seeking energy has dissolved since meeting you. We are here together for a purpose, and I feel that is to reawaken light within Atlantis and our people. I also feel there is much for us to explore within each other that will bring abundance to our spiritual knowledge and understanding. I don't truly know our purpose or what we have to instigate; however, I do feel a longing within my being to remain with you so that we can truly discover the guidance and divine plan of our souls, the Celestial White Beings, and the Creator." Benjamin's voice was so gentle that I felt as if my soul was drinking it in.

I was tired after the transmission of the Celestial White Beings. I wanted to agree with Benjamin, but I found myself roaming between meditation and sleep. Feeling my body relax further, I left meditation behind and quickly drifted into a sleep state.

Nara's Notes

The angelic kingdom constantly reminds us of the divine presence within our beings with its beautiful qualities of love, truth, peace, bliss, and much more. The angels emanate to us unconditional and selfless love so that we might believe the same exists within us. When we can radiate the divine within us, which could be likened to radiating the vibration of love, we realize there is no room for the ego — no space to believe we are right or wrong, to be fearful or overpowering, to manipulate, or to not act. When love emanates, freedom, expansion, and the feeling of sharing arise. The angels teach us to love ourselves unconditionally, believing we are special and valued and can accept our own power without coming from a place of ego.

Practice 12
Breathe with the Angels

Out loud, invite your personal angels to surround you with their unconditional and selfless love. It doesn't matter if you are aware of them or not.

Imagine, sense, or acknowledge that you are breathing the light and love vibration of your angels into your entire being. Especially let their energy ride the flow of your breath.

Your focus is to experience, sense, or be aware of the love around you while feeling it form and build within your being. There are many sensations associated with this: joy, warmth, and even the experience of an opening in the heart chakra. It can be immensely healing.

Allow the practice of focusing on your breath and the presence of love to encourage a perspective, understanding, and experience of merging. You and the angels' vibrations are becoming one; there is no separation. This can take you into a deep state of love, which you can experience for as long as you wish. Remember to send the energy of love through your feet into the earth to complete the process, grounding yourself back in your reality when you are ready.

Practice 13
Share the Love of the Creator

This is an opportunity to share the love of the Creator throughout your daily routine. When you connect or come in contact with a person, it is customary to offer a spoken greeting. I ask you, whether you offer a spoken greeting or not, to encourage yourself to enter a pattern of igniting love within your being, allowing it to exude like a spotlight from your heart center in the direction of the person. You could describe it as an energetic greeting; in truth, you are activating the divine within your being and openly showing this to the other person, even though that person might not be consciously aware. This will develop into your being able to resonate with, connect to, and sense the truth of the other person, therefore creating an energetic union. If it is the divine plan of the Creator for you to converse with the other person or for some synchronicity to arise, everything will be borne from a pure vibration. If you continue your journey, then you have connected with an aspect of the Creator, accepting the Creator in this other person while acknowledging the Creator within your being. In many ways, your spiritual awakening is all about remembrance. To remember the divine within you, repeated focus is needed to re-form a natural pattern of connecting with the Creator.

To achieve this, simply inhale while focusing in your heart chakra on the vibration of love. Exhale while allowing the energy to emanate in the direction of your choosing. It can be as quick and as easy as that.

This practice will encourage you to be alert and aware of your surroundings. Does a tree, flower, animal, insect, water, or the wind deserve your recognition and love? Are they aspects of the Creator? I believe so.

Practice 14
Breathe with a Tree

I encourage you to find a tree and to stand beyond the length of its branches. First call on the protection of Archangel Michael, and then place both hands on your heart.

Inhale, activating and focusing on the love of the Creator within your being. Exhale, sending your love to the tree.

Ask within your mind if you are permitted to commune with the tree and to enter its auric field. An answer can manifest as a thought, sensation, or simple knowingness. Only commune with a tree that is open to your presence.

Place your right hand on the tree trunk while keeping your left hand on your heart center. This is to remind you of all intentions flowing from a space of purity and love within your being.

Begin to breathe as one with the tree. Inhale, holding the intention of accepting the highest positive vibrations of love from the tree. Let its energy flow as if on your breath into your being.

Exhale, emanating your own vibration of love on your breath and from every aspect of your being into the tree. Continue this process.

As you allow yourself to focus more on the rhythm and energy exchange you are creating, you might gradually feel yourself becoming one with the tree. You will unite your energies, increasing each other's vibrational speed and thus allowing yourself to enter a greater realization of light.

When you wish to complete the process, simply remove your hand and concentrate on your feet being firmly planted in the ground.

7

Jacob's Ascension

Benjamin and I slept under the tree throughout the night, comforted by each other's energies and supported by the presence of the enlightened tree. The time had passed so quickly that our souls wished for the time of stillness together to rejuvenate our energy matrix systems and exchange vital consciousness. The Celestial White Beings were aligning us both to a quicker frequency and vibration of their energy, therefore allowing them to communicate and connect with us with greater ease. It also allowed Benjamin and me to feel a spiritual closeness as we began to develop our abilities to work together. It was akin to a divine map being formed within our energies and the universe, allowing synchronicities to roll into place. By being together, we were accepting the roles our souls wished to play on Atlantis.

Waking from my deep and peaceful sleep, I gently stirred Benjamin with my movement. The sun was rising in the sky in preparation for a beautifully warm day, and the tall green grass surrounding the tree glistened. Benjamin looked radiantly at me, his eyes so filled with the love of the Creator that I almost could not gaze into them, yet a part of me longed to.

"I wish to return to the temple," I said abruptly.

"As you wish," Benjamin said, rising to his feet. "May I accompany you?"

"I suppose so." An awkward feeling was growing within me, and I felt as if I wanted to push Benjamin away and rest in my own energies.

We began to walk side by side back through the tall grass, slowly moving up the hill as we weaved through the trees along the path we had run down with such a sense of freedom the night before. Silence fell between us, but it was no longer a peace of being at one with each other; it was a stillness that seemed to manifest as a barrier of separation.

"You are unsettled?" Benjamin quietly asked, hoping to encourage me to express my thoughts.

"When you connect with the Creator or the Celestial White Beings, do you experience a love that is encompassing, nurturing, and expansive, that completely fills your entire being and senses? A love you do not recognize as yourself but you know deep within you is everything you are and is more truthful than anything on Earth? This experience of love as I connect with the Creator is so profound and has grown with time and dedication. I know I can just allow the love of the Creator, which is my own, to flow from my being. It doesn't require me to act in any way while guiding me to act according to the will of the Creator.

"Benjamin, I have the same experience when I connect with your energies or am in your presence. I have always felt a love flowing from me to loved ones and those around me, and when I am with you, it is as if I have a fuller and more complete experience of the Creator without the need to meditate or focus myself spiritually. I am not really sure what this means. Are we supposed to be like brother and sister? Partners or lovers? I have never experienced this feeling of being so connected to the universe due to the presence of another physical being. I am at a loss of how to act and react in your presence." My words escaped me quickly as I tried to express the jumbled thoughts in my mind.

"I do understand, Nara," Benjamin shared, watching me intently as I sighed with relief. "We are akin to brother and sister. We are family, yet we can — if we wish — be lovers on Earth. There are many opportunities available to us in this moment. The key, as you know, is to follow your inner guidance. Do what feels most natural and comfortable to you. Do not act from fear; act from love, and see where you are guided. Our relationship is an adventure, because when we are exploring each other's energies, we are actually exploring our selves as the Creator.

"What is occurring between us seems unique, but I believe this is the way everyone on Atlantis is meant to exist. With open hearts to love each other, knowing whether we are alone or in the presence of others, we can experience a fuller, more complete aspect of our selves as the Creator. Our experience might be of greater intensity because we are from the same soul group and have journeyed together many times. We also have a purpose, so our guides are pouring light into our reality in support. Nara, the Celestial White Beings spoke of this through you last night — the experience of unity through the Creator's love — because we all recognize and truly believe every soul on Earth is an expression of the Creator.

We have all known this since our birth; however, we are now experiencing it at a higher frequency and level to embody the experience more fully.

"Nara, be as you are, as you feel, and as you are guided. Let yourself be free. Do not restrict yourself through your thoughts. I will do the same. Remember, we are mirrors for each other, so that which occurs within you is present within me and vice versa. It is the same for any relationship, connection, or observation with another being." Benjamin fell silent as the glistening white beacon temple came into view.

"Thank you for the reminder, Benjamin. I realize my energy vibration has quickened, so I am aligned more fully with all aspects of the Creator. I feel, through meeting you, I have accepted and adopted a new way of existing with people on Earth, a way of being united with them in their presence and acknowledging the familiarity and similarities between us. It is a profound growth and awakening within my being that allows me to remember myself more fully as the Creator." In my heart, I experienced a guided sensation that inspired me to reach out and hold Benjamin's hand as we walked the final steps to the temple.

Gazing up at my beautiful temple, which always filled me with joy when I approached it, I experienced a start as I saw Jacob resting on his side before the temple door. My heart began to race, and I released Benjamin's hand as I ran to Jacob's side. I had been waiting for this time and knew with a slight sense of dread what was about to unfold.

"It is time, Nara," Jacob telepathically spoke to me as I clutched his neck, pressing my face against his gray coat.

"Jacob, can you stand? I would like to move you into the temple so you can be supported by its energy network," I spoke telepathically.

Benjamin used his strength to help the horse to his feet. With Jacob's cooperation, we slowly and carefully walked him into the center of the temple, where he could rest on the marble floor.

"You can hear our telepathic conversation?" I questioned Benjamin.

"Yes, of course. Every thought we have can be heard by the universe and all souls. If we recognize ourselves as the universe and the Creator, we can hear everything. Is he ascending?"

"Yes, I think so." I had not realized Benjamin and I were speaking without sound.

After grasping two cushions from the pile at the door of the temple, I threw one to Benjamin. We sat down with Benjamin behind Jacob and me in front so that I could look into Jacob's eyes as he lay on his side. Breathing deeply, we asked to connect with Jacob's soul and the divine plan for Jacob in that moment. We asked to be of service and to be guided as to how we could support Jacob. Archangel Michael came into our awareness.

"Beloved Nara and Benjamin, please know I, Archangel Michael, am here to support you. Jacob has chosen for you both to be present at his ascension and is grateful for the role you are now playing. Jacob's time on Earth is coming to an end; he has mastered and learned all his soul required to attain, realizing himself as the Creator more fully. Through his learning — which has been inspired by you, Nara — he has now broken away from the cycle of rebirth, which means he has no need to return to Earth. It is time for him to depart from Earth, as his energies are needed on the inner planes to play an important role in the reality unfolding for both of you.

"Nara, your connection with Jacob means he will be able to guide you with tremendous power and influence in your future. Jacob will enter the realms of the unicorn kingdom and become a unicorn guide holding a similar vibration to that of the angelic kingdom.

"While many people can remain in their physical bodies as they attain and realize enlightenment, love consciousness, mind mastery, freedom, and union with the Creator, Jacob is needed on the inner planes and so has chosen to leave his body on his ascension. You can see his body is now weakening; the functions of many of his organs are slowing as the light and essence of his being, which you know as his soul, prepares to withdraw from his physical body. Do not be concerned. Jacob is not in pain. His focus is now on his essence. In this space, there is no pain — only love and nourishment." Archangel Michael informed us of this with his gentle and protective energy, and his presence seemed to embrace the three of us.

The Celestial White Beings were anchoring to the temple, their white-mist light energy cascading from the crystal embedded above us. They spiraled their energy to create a column of light around us that extended up into the heavens.

I gently caressed Jacob's neck and mane, his velvety warm body familiar to my touch. He was my friend, a true companion I would miss dearly. I could feel tears welling up and rolling down my cheeks. I knew Jacob would be safe and that it was his destiny to move into the light, leaving his physical body behind; however, I could feel the pain of his loss burning in my heart and a reluctance to let him go.

Jacob was a source of happiness and had been there in my times of loneliness. He dissolved the pain of my loneliness and without his presence, a part of me felt that loneliness might return. Before I sank deeper into my emotions, I realized loneliness was an aspect of my past. I had learned to more fully experience the love of no longer feeling separated from the Creator. I recognized that to support Jacob's ascension, I had to detach from his energy and let him go. This would make the shift easier for both of us. My final recognition helped me realize I would always be able to connect with Jacob, communicating and uniting our energies as one. There was no separation between us — only a shift, an alteration and a change in our existence together. I inhaled deeply with a powerful focus and intention in my mind, which resonated with my entire being, of dissolving all bonds of attachment with Jacob. I exhaled, knowing in the moment I had let him go. With my next inhalation, I accepted that holding on to Jacob was only a manifestation of fear and a desire to be in control, disregarding the Creator's divine will. To be as the Creator on Earth is not about control, manipulation, or dictating to others; it is to allow the Creator to work through you as you exist in a humble, loving space. I was surrendering to the Creator, which was what the Creator asked of Jacob in that moment.

"You are safe and able to surrender fully in this moment to exist in harmony with the Creator," I whispered to Jacob.

"Thank you, Nara. You have played your role beautifully by following the guidance within you and without my intervention," Archangel Michael confirmed. "Jacob understands how he can make his ascension path now. It would encourage his release if you were to play a supportive role. You can connect to his energy by imagining or being aware of his light expanding and surrendering to merge with the energy of the Creator. With the integration of his own soul light and the Creator within his physical body, he can now surrender into the space of the Creator. With your support and the presence of the angelic kingdom, he will let go of his earthly reality and body, moving completely into the light and dimensions of the unicorn kingdom — completely leaving his body." Archangel Michael's transmission was inspiring our minds.

Closing our eyes, we expanded the love of our essence within our being to merge with Jacob's auric field and then his soul light, which we connected with at his heart center. White pearlescent light filled my senses as all colors of the rainbow greeted me on a backdrop of white. Jacob's energy was increasing in speed and intensifying in beauty with every moment. I acknowledged the light of the Creator, which seemed divinely pure as it flowed into Jacob's being and embraced his soul light. I could see from behind my closed eyelids that the temple was flooded with brilliant and dazzling light as two aspects of the Creator reunited. I cried in bliss and happiness; Jacob's soul reunion with the Creator was *our* reunion with the Creator, as we are as one — always connected with everything. I experienced the

Creator's vibrations flow deeper into my own being, encouraging me to surrender to the light as a consequence of being in Jacob's presence. I felt as if I was soaring high, and yet I was still aware of Jacob's experience.

There was a bright flash of light — as if the vibrancy of that light had been strengthened 1,000 times — and then the light vanished. Opening my eyes quickly, I saw Jacob's last breath leave his body, and then he was at peace. I instinctively placed my hand on Jacob's heart center to send love through his heart to accompany his soul as it rose through the dimensions of the Creator.

An image entered my mind like a flash of lightning: Jacob was standing tall and more radiant than ever. His coat was absolutely white, and his eyes glowed with a rainbow light. An energetic spiral of light — his new unicorn horn — extended from his third-eye chakra. Jacob emitted bliss, happiness, and joy.

"I have returned home," he said. He was now in full remembrance and experience of the Creator as well as the world beyond Earth. I placed my third eye against his lifeless body and gave thanks for this most beautiful and inspirational blessing.

It took Benjamin and me some time to recover from the energy vibrations that had stimulated us. We stayed in stillness for a while to pay homage to Jacob and all involved while grounding ourselves back into the earth and reality. Later, with the help of the community members, we set Jacob's body on a raft to freely move with the current of the ocean. We all watched in awe, gratitude, and togetherness with great elation as his body floated toward the setting sun, a glowing red ball gradually drifting into the sea. Jacob's ascension brought forth a great sense of inspiration and completion for our community.

Nara's Notes

When you dedicate yourself to existing with a spiritual perspective, there is always a sense that you're part of a great unfolding journey, an adventure in a world that includes and expands beyond Earth. Synchronicities and miracles, as well as being in the right place at the right time, are a part of being in the divine flow of the Creator; each experience enhances your conscious awareness of the Creator, which feels like magic. I have spoken of the experience of a divine plan unfolding and guiding you forth, but you should also grasp that by supporting others and allowing a sacred connection with those around you, your experience of the Creator intensifies as you acknowledge the Creator within everything and everyone. When we recognize the Creator in others, we also accept the same within ourselves.

Ascension can have many names and pathways with diverse teachings. To me, ascension is a process of surrendering to the Creator, accessing your remembrance of the Creator, and embodying Its pure vibrations within your being and reality. Essentially, it is not about leaving Earth and your physical body but achieving a state of awareness of the truth within and around you, which allows you to exist in harmony with yourself along with everyone and everything. Any person, animal, or being can ascend; we are all ascending continuously.

In truth, Jacob's ascension did not occur in the moment he fully surrendered to the Creator and left his body. It was his soul's entire journey through different lifetimes — every moment of awareness — that was his ascension path and process. Every moment of our awareness truly is divine and precious.

Practice 15
Ascension Accompanied by Your Unicorn Guide

A unicorn is a symbol of enlightenment in the same way an angel can be the symbol of unconditional love. They are beings who exist on the same vibration and dimensions as the angelic kingdom. Some unicorns have existed on Earth as horses, while others have only existed within the inner planes. The greatest tool of a unicorn is its energy horn that protrudes from its third eye chakra at its brow; it is a tool to aid the synthesis and manifestation of light. Unicorns represent the Creator's vibration of purity and can help us experience the innocence of our souls, enabling us to accept our truth and develop sacred practices of purification.

If you wish to connect with the unicorn vibrations, then you can call forth a unicorn to join your community of guides who support your spiritual awakening. Some people already unconsciously have invoked unicorns to be instrumental within their reality. Whether you have or not, calling forth the most appropriate unicorn guide to accompany you will unite you with the unicorn vibrations.

CONNECTION

First, create a space of peace and stillness within and around your being by breathing deeply and relaxing your body. Say out loud,

From a space of love within my being and the inner planes, I invoke the most appropriate unicorn being to step forward to become my unicorn guide. Make me aware of your presence as I open my heart to connect and accept you with love. Thank you.

You may or may not become aware of your unicorn guide instantly. Know you are being surrounded by its energy, which you are connecting with through your focused breathing. You might gain insights, visions, or words, and you might even ask for your unicorn guide's name. Allow yourself to be free to explore. Remember, there is a need for you to trust in your abilities to communicate and to receive energy vibrations and consciousness.

PURIFICATION

Whether you are aware of your unicorn guide or not, ask it to place its horn into the right and then the left chakras of your hands, creating puddles of pearlescent light within each chakra.

Move your hands to your crown chakra at the top of your head, and imagine the light transferring from your hand chakras into your crown chakra. This is a process of purifying and cleansing your chakras while also encouraging you to attune with and remember the vibration of the unicorn kingdom, which is an expression of the Creator.

Bring your hands down, and imagine the unicorn is dipping its energetic horn into your right and then left hand chakras, filling the chakras with pearlescent light. Move your hands to the front — and if possible, the back — of your third eye chakra at your brow, holding the focus of the energy transferring into the chakra for a healing, balancing, and purifying experience.

Repeat this process with your throat chakra, heart chakra

(in your chest center), solar plexus chakra (just above the waist), sacral chakra (just below the waist), and root chakra (at the base of your spine). As the light enters your root chakra, feel or guide the light to flow down your legs and out through your feet chakras into the earth.

Permit the unicorn to channel its light into the chakras of your hands once more, creating two stars of light.

Reach your right hand up and your left hand down. Imagine the stars simultaneously flowing into your soul star chakra above your head, which assists in filtering your soul light, and your earth star chakra below your feet, which then aids in the grounding and manifestation of the Creator within your reality.

Focus for a moment on all your chakras experiencing vibrations of purity being cleansed, healed, and balanced to exist in harmony.

INNOCENCE
Say out loud,

I invite my unicorn guide to place its unicorn horn within my heart chakra with the intention to activate the innocence, essence, and purity of my heart and soul into manifestation within my reality and awareness. Work with me to aid my greater awareness of the truth within my being so that I may access this understanding daily. Thank you.

Allow yourself to trust in the energy of the unicorn awakening vibrations within you.

MANIFESTATION
Say out loud,

I invite my unicorn guide to place its energetic horn and vibration within my third eye chakra. I ask for my third eye chakra to be cleansed. Please empower my abilities of manifestation. Together let us cocreate an intention and reality of me walking my ascension pathways with ease, perfection, precision, and awareness, grasping and understanding new and old lessons of growth and dissolving all unneeded energetic patterns, habits, and creations as well as encouraging my greater unity with all that is the Creator. Thank you, and so it is.

Give time for your unicorn to work with your third eye chakra, and allow yourself to focus on your intentions for your ascension and spiritual growth process in this reality. Let all thoughts of manifestation be borne from love.

Know you may call on your unicorn guide whenever you wish; even thinking of your unicorn guide allows you to connect. Your unicorn guide is ready to accompany you through your journey of spiritual awakening.

CHAPTER

8

Reunion

From my home nestled in the woods between the temple and our community, I made my way to my parents' house in the very center of the village. The sun was beginning to set, casting a bright pink light across the sky as if a painter had been at work all day creating a masterpiece on the horizon. I was excited about visiting Martyna and Parlo, as they had invited Benjamin and me to dinner in celebration of our growing union. My heart felt open and expansive; as I walked through nature, every moment felt like a magnificent and sacredly precious time. Everything seemed to fill me with glee, even the most mundane things. I had chosen to wear a dark blue tunic with turquoise crystals delicately interlaced into the fabric. I allowed my pale red hair to flow over my right shoulder with dainty pink flowers plaited through my waves.

As I drew close to my family and birth home — the beautiful house nestled in a majestic tree — I noticed my parents sitting at a table in the garden, intensely connecting and communicating with Benjamin. I stopped at the edge of their garden, camouflaged by the trees, to take in the picture before me. Martyna was facing me with her elbow on the table, resting her chin in her hand as she gazed at Benjamin and nodded every so often in agreement. Her bright red curly hair cascaded down her back and over one shoulder as she tried to bat her thick locks back. Her build was slight, her skin pale, and her lips as red as her hair; her character was fiery, and yet her overall radiance was of compassion to every being, including herself. Candles cast light on their animated faces as they spoke.

My father sat next to his wife. His strong build, light brown hair, and deep brown eyes emitted a dashing look. He wore a bright yellow tunic and exuded openness, acceptance, and friendship — the qualities of his character. Both my parents were wiser than they shared, with the ability to understand more about a person's energies and divine plan than they declared.

Wearing a pale-green tunic, Benjamin had his back to me, but I could sense he was content in the presence of my parents.

Parlo looked in my direction, scanning with his physical eyes and his third eye. He had obviously sensed my presence, so I emerged from the trees, walking quickly in their direction. I was happy to join them, as the atmosphere they had created was one warmth and joy.

"Nara!" Parlo shouted, jumping up to embrace me in his bear-like hug. "We have been anticipating your arrival." He released me to allow Martyna to delicately hold me for a few moments, her pale pink tunic billowing around me.

"We have been discovering past-life and sacred inner-plane school connections with Benjamin. It is very enlightening. It seems we have studied with similar masters on the inner planes, such as Isis and Master Kuthumi. It has been wonderful to speak of such things, as it brings their energy to intertwine within our gathering." Martyna's face was filled with delight.

I moved toward Benjamin, but we didn't speak. He simply placed his lips on my cheek in a deeply loving caress. The union between us was intensifying; I could feel my inner strength growing with his presence.

"I am so pleased to see you, Nara," he telepathically beamed to me. I smiled with warmth in return and sat down next to him at the table.

I saw in the candlelight that the table was covered with wooden plates of delicious food so brightly colored that they looked like the essence of a rainbow. The multicolored vegetables and fruits Martyna had prepared made my stomach rumble with anticipation.

Parlo poured some water into wooden containers for each of us. We began by individually expressing our thanks to Mother Earth, the elementals, and the Creator for the food we were about to consume. Our prayers were silent but filled with gratitude and love, which seeped into the food and charged it with positive vibrations to be returned to our bodies as we ate. I knew our food already held a high concentration of love because Martyna had cared for the fruit and vegetables with her own hands in her garden.

When I was a child, I often found my mother talking to her plants, filling them with love and encouraging them to grow in health and vitality. I was brought up on vegetables, fruits, nuts, and seeds, and when I entered my teenage years, my parents taught me to nourish my body with light alone so that I wouldn't require food.

They taught me to meditate a few times a day using special advanced rhythmic breathing patterns to absorb greater volumes of light with the intention of my body receiving all the nurturance it requires to exist in health and vivacity. This took some time to master; my body went through stages of starvation until I mastered the technique and erased the natural programming of the physical body's need for food to survive.

For our family, sitting down to eat food together meant it was a real celebration. An air of merriment circulated around and through our beings as we rejoiced in each other's company, passing plates back and forth with discussions of our favorite dishes. We chatted about life at the temple, Martyna's vegetable garden, and news within the community, as well as the animals and birds we had seen lately while walking in nature. It was after we had explored these subjects that Martyna approached a new subject, which was, in fact, her reason for inviting Benjamin and me to be with them this evening.

"Nara, upon your birth, the priestesses accessed your soul's divine plan for your current lifetime. As you know, they supported you by anchoring all you would require energetically to achieve your divine purpose on Atlantis. I have not told you that the priestesses asked your soul if there was anything Parlo and I needed to know to support you in your reality. Before leaving our home in central Atlantis, a priestess who was my most trusted friend and companion in prayer and communion with the Creator handed me a scroll that I have treasured and safeguarded all these years. Handwritten by the priestess on the scroll are specific guidelines from your soul."

Martyna paused a moment and produced a small, tanned scroll in perfect condition, which she then unrolled and placed on the table, holding the edges firmly to keep the scroll from recoiling.

"I feel it is now time for me to share this sacred guidance with you in the company of your loved ones." Martyna's eyes shifted down to study the scroll.

The language on the scroll was one I had not seen before. Some words resembled other languages my parents had taught me, but I couldn't make out the wisdom on the scroll even though I squinted to scan it methodically. The presence of the scroll and the meaning or influence it might have on my current reality baffled me.

"I do not recognize the language," I finally confessed.

"It is the light language of the Celestial White Beings from the fourteenth dimension. They have other light languages at different dimensions beyond that, but they have not taught you their fourteenth-dimensional language because it would unlock many sources of wisdom from their presence. This would cause you to become lost in exploration of their energy and the universe when their wish for you is to be grounded in your Atlantean reality as an anchor for their vibration, enabling them to transmit their and your Creator aspect and truth to all souls."

Martyna gazed hopefully at me, and I could sense she was hoping I wouldn't be offended by this information.

"But you can read the language?" I asked, trying to remain in a state of acceptance rather than feeling excluded.

"When I first opened the scroll when you were only a baby, the language was downloaded instantly into my consciousness so that I could interpret it to you in this moment. I have been studying the scrolls with much dedication to ensure my translation is the purest," Martyna reassured me.

"Please read the scroll to us." My encouragement came from a state of profound peace. Martyna nodded gratefully and inhaled to center herself before she began.

"Your soul speaks of a long period of peace and preparation designed to offer you time to nurture the embodiment of your soul within your being — a time when you, as a spiritual and divine being, can enjoy the life Atlantis has to offer. This period is a gift to you because of the work you have achieved in previous lifetimes and because of the mission your soul has contracted in the later part of your life in this reality. Your soul speaks of sacred reunion, unconditional love, and unity with a man who is your equal and soul mate — born from the same soul group as you. Your soul names this being Benjamin."

Martyna looked up at Benjamin, studying his expression for a moment. He simply held an expression of knowingness.

"It is required that your reunion be marked with a blessing, as this symbolizes a major shift in the soul group of the Celestial White Beings, allowing their energy to expand and permeate Earth with tremendous force. The blessing will also symbolize a call for help from Atlantis to the inner planes and heavens — our home. Nara and Benjamin, your reunion was always going to take place; however, the timing is significant because, like two magnets, you will be attracted together when Atlantis reaches a pinnacle of its journey: either to fall from a lack of love or to continue, accepting love. If you allow the blessing to take place, you will allow

Atlantis and the general consciousness of Atlantis to receive sacred blessings of harmonious vibrations to support the vibration of love within each of us.

"You both also contracted to experience some forms of chaos and will accept the negative influences, acting as healing beacons to transform the energies into love. Nara, your soul speaks of many people on Atlantis who have contracted to accept the karma of the Atlantean people, as they are equipped to release and heal it on behalf of all. Both of you have contracted to dissolve the karma of Atlantis, but Nara, your soul warns you not to become distracted by or attached to the chaos by believing it is your own, as this could then carry into other lifetimes on Earth.

"Your presence together now symbolizes that disharmony is manifesting on Atlantis, and it could be journeying to a fall in its vibration. Your soul doesn't say how chaos or the fall of Atlantis might manifest, but your soul wishes you to know your reunion with Benjamin is a new beginning that offers a second chance to Atlanteans, as enormous volumes of love will be anchored to heal all. This is truly a blessing. At this time, your soul asks you to surrender to your path and its guidance, as you are now truly entering a time of service."

Martyna fell silent, scanning the scroll to see whether she missed anything.

"What of your role as parents?" Benjamin asked.

"In truth, it only asks Parlo and me to support you both by following our inner guidance and to remain in high vibration, not allowing our minds or emotions to be influenced by outside experiences or situations. This is something we have based our parenthood practice on. We hope to continue offering our wisdom and strength to you both. I have waited for this moment, knowing its importance while not wishing to face the reality of chaos emerging on Atlantis," Martyna replied honestly.

Parlo placed his arm around Martyna to comfort her.

"It is already here, my dear. It was one of the reasons we moved to this safe haven. It has been like a serpent, gently uncoiling, unnoticed by most — until finally we recognize its power. We are being warned and have been warned for some time. Now is the time to confront fear; after all, chaos is born from fear alone."

"A message filled with love, hope, and sadness. There seems to be so much hidden wisdom within those words. I find myself asking, 'Why me? Why am I special?' I know Hamna would tell me I am not special and to simply put myself forward to achieve a role that many have similarly achieved."

I laughed out loud, knowing Hamna's perspective to be true. I experienced a strength growing in me like a rod of steel, which I had not previously experienced. I turned to Benjamin and gazed into his beautiful, loving eyes.

"I would like very much for our reunion to be blessed and for us to exist as companions of love, moving through our reality together. I wish to surrender to you — not because I know it will support Atlantis, but because I accept you as an aspect of myself. As I see the beauty of you, I recognize the grace of my own being and soul. What do you wish for?"

Every part of my being was beaming with love as if every cell was smiling broadly. Benjamin laughed with compassion and joy.

"I could not think of anything better. Let us bring forth vibrations of celebration and joy. Let us encourage love to fill the air!"

Benjamin scooped me into his arms, holding me tightly as he danced around the garden and laughed in ecstasy and joy.

"I will begin preparations for the blessing," Martyna excitedly announced as we returned to the table.

"Please do," I confirmed, laughing. However, something else was on my mind. "There is a more sinister note in the message, isn't there? I find it so hard to imagine Atlantis falling and chaos being born when our community is like a sanctuary, so filled with love and high vibrations. I have never been to any other part of Atlantis, but in a naive way, I perceive all communities to be as ours." I smiled meekly.

"It is why we and many other people were sent from central Atlantis into the countryside," Parlo reminded us. "It was to preserve the treasures of wisdom, consciousness, connection, and sacred abilities that have been discovered through spiritual exploration within the temples. We are Guardians of the Truth, our own inner truth, which is the essence of the Creator. We are all beacons of Atlantis."

"Do we know what is happening to Atlantis? How will chaos materialize?" I asked.

"Hamna has been trying to discover what is occurring by telepathically speaking to many who are closer to the center. All he can understand is that fear and separation are manifesting."

We each knew the power of fear and separation within our own beings and wondered how this would manifest if a large proportion of our civilization were creating it. The energy of our group began to lower in vibration as visions of fear and separation manifesting physically within Atlantis passed through our minds.

Benjamin gazed at me with love.

"It is not for us to wonder or to think of. It is for us to remain in a state of love. Our blessing will remind us all of love." He renewed the love within us all with his words of reassurance.

Our evening continued, bubbling with excitement as we discussed plans for the blessing and enjoyed each other's company.

Nara's Notes

The discovery of the scroll awakened within Benjamin and me a deep strength, power, and knowingness of our purpose on Earth to serve the Creator, the Celestial White Beings, and the souls incarnate on Atlantis. Our conscious awareness of the services we would offer was very poor, yet it felt as if our souls were building within us in preparation for the moments to come. It is in this moment of my sharing with you that I wish to begin to awaken within you the remembrance of your own Atlantean self, encouraging you to connect with this aspect of your being to access appropriate memories and understandings. While gaining a wider picture and understanding of your own Atlantean experience is important, I wish to focus first on reconnecting you with the energies of Atlantis and then, gradually, your Atlantean self.

Imagine a bubble. This represents your soul group, which is an extension of the Creator. From this bubble, twelve bubbles are formed, and one of these twelve extensions from your soul group is your soul. Your soul, like the other eleven souls, creates twelve more extensions.

You are one of twelve extensions from your soul. The other soul extensions may exist on Earth or stars or other planets in the universe of the Creator. There are numerous soul groups expanding in this way to more fully experience the essence of the Creator.

As an extension of your soul, your purpose is to embody that soul to allow integration with it and its other eleven extensions, thus returning to oneness with your truth. As a soul extension, you have numerous lifetimes on Earth and the inner planes; however, in each lifetime, different qualities are drawn from your soul and recorded — almost as characters — within the soul. You might also be able to access the lifetimes of the other eleven extensions of your soul, even remembering them as your own.

Each lifetime is experienced simultaneously, as time doesn't exist. Lifetime experiences can filter into other lifetimes; this is when you perceive you are remembering past lifetimes. Therefore, your Atlantean lifetime is occurring now, but in your current reality, you perceive it as in the past.

Your Atlantean lifetime demonstrates qualities and aspects of your soul akin to seeing a different side of yourself. Often, aspects of the soul require healing and therefore step forward into your current reality for completion and understanding. Connecting with past-lifetime aspects can allow you to recognize patterns within your reality borne from a previous lifetime. It is most likely that your soul wishes you to discover or heal aspects of your Atlantean self to enrich your current reality; this may be why you have been drawn to connect with my energies. We might have held a connection in Atlantis — or not. It does not matter either way, as that which is appropriate for you to discover will be revealed to you.

Practice 16
Trust and Hold Faith

When wishing to gain inspiration and remembrance from your soul and past lifetimes, there is a tool that will assist you tremendously in receiving wisdom. This tool is your trust, belief, and faith in yourself. Often the first statement made by many when they wish to receive remembrance is a focus on their perceived inability — their disbelief or doubt in the process and their own abilities — to receive. The more confidence you have in your ability to receive wisdom, along with placing trust in the understanding you gain (if it resonates with you), the easier you will find the entire experience. In many ways, no one can truly understand the lifetimes of your soul other than you. Others will describe what they see or maybe feel, interpreting you from their own experiences, but you have direct access to your experiences and can even relive them. Trust, faith, and belief in yourself and your abilities naturally exist within your being, within the energy you might recognize as your spiritual energetic power.

Your trust, faith, and belief can be eroded and disempowered, however, through the negative statements others share with you or through negative thoughts you choose to create and empower with repetition. You still hold trust, faith, and belief, but you have chosen to fuel negative doubts about yourself rather than stimulate empowering thoughts with the same energies. With this in mind, I wish to share with you an affirmation to empower your reconnection with the energies of trust, faith, and belief to focus them positively.

Imagine within your solar plexus chakra (above your waist) a deep glowing flame of light. Let the flame be a color that represents trust, faith, and belief to you. The flame is akin to fuel, a nourishing power holding the qualities of your self-trust, faith, and belief. Allow yourself to accept this affirmation:

I completely and absolutely trust, hold faith, and believe in myself and my abilities as a divine being.

If you choose to simply read the words over and over or if you affirm with your eyes closed, imagine the flame at your solar plexus grows with each repetition. Let the flame become so powerful it encompasses you completely.

When you feel you have completed this process, ask for your chakras to be balanced. You will fill with the power of trust, faith, and belief.

In your reality, notice when you doubt or lose faith in yourself or your abilities. Then remember this meditation and affirmation, linking into your inner power of positive trust, faith, and belief in all you are and what you can achieve.

Practice 17
Establish an Atlantean Connection

Take a few deep breaths, and allow yourself to relax into a state of meditation and peace. Say out loud,

I now invoke the angels of Atlantis and Nara Merlyn to draw close into my auric field, surrounding me completely in the energy and vibration of love. I ask you to transport me to the Celestial White Beings' temple on the northern side of Atlantis so that I may begin to reconnect with or become aware of my Atlantean energies. Thank you.

Breathe in the light surrounding you, imagining, acknowledging, or knowing you are entering the temple surrounded completely by the pure white light of the Celestial White Beings. Let yourself be aware of your surroundings as you breathe deeply. Say out loud,

I ask to receive, if divinely appropriate, the love vibration of Atlantis and the love many beings on Atlantis held for my Atlantean self. Let even the love vibration held within my Atlantean self awaken within my conscious awareness and feelings as I receive love from all directions penetrating into my being while simultaneously awakening from within my being. I allow myself to experience the love vibration of Atlantis. Thank you.

Simply sit with the focus of receiving and experiencing love, recognizing or observing new vibrations or insights that come into your awareness.

This practice creates a strong foundation for your present self and Atlantean self to connect and communicate while also supporting Atlantis. Remember, everything is occurring simultaneously. With your presence and connection into Atlantis focusing on love, you are boosting the love vibration of Atlantis and its general consciousness.

You might gain glimpses of your Atlantean self, but try to simply focus on receiving love. We will explore a further connection later.

Experience this practice for as long and as many times as feels appropriate. When you wish to return to your current reality, simply ask the angels of Atlantis[1] to ground you back in your physical life. Then focus on breathing light into the earth through your feet to complete your grounding process.

---

1   The angels of Atlantis are angels who were present and supported the Atlantean civilization. They are guardians of the Atlantean wisdom, consciousness, love, and light. It is often through and with the support of the angels of Atlantis that you can connect on a deeper level with the spiritual teachings of Atlantis and your Atlantean experiences.

CHAPTER

9

Bluebell's Plea

The sound of trickling water filled my senses as I sat cross-legged on a protruding stone in the center of a small river. I had stumbled on this sacred space just outside our community, on the southern side, many years ago. It was a place I visited when I wanted to ground myself and purify my energies. The sound and vibration of the water stimulated my senses with a refreshing energy that denoted a new beginning for myself in my reality. I would soon begin a new existence as Benjamin's partner and wished to prepare myself on all levels of my being to welcome change free from fear and embraced in love. The water seemed to carry away all aspects, perspectives, and habits I had only recently recognized as myself in order for the new empowered aspect of myself that I had chosen to acknowledge to step forth. Each stage of our reality requires us to let go of who we truly believe ourselves to be and embrace aspects that will support our experiences ahead.

I imagined myself to be a crystalline being of glistening pure white light growing constantly in strength and inner power. I felt more grounded in my true self than I had ever previously experienced. Power grew with intensity from within my soul, and it felt as if I was becoming physically taller while I sensed a tremendous weighty sensation of being worthy of all that the Creator wished to provide to me. Empowerment was my overall feeling, and this was the reason I had been drawn to this sacred space. It was time for me to accept and realize my inner power, knowing there was nothing within or around me that could diminish it.

I knew that my soul and the Creator wished for Benjamin and me to experience a unity of our energies, and I realized for this to take place, I needed to exist in a space within myself that was grounded in my own power, ensuring any needed healing had taken place and my love for myself was strong. This way, I would not try to seek from Benjamin energies and feelings that I must activate within myself, nor would I give my power away to Benjamin by allowing him to make choices for me against my will or by believing we are not equal. I knew the greatest gift I could share with Benjamin and myself was empowerment of my love for myself before I shared my love with him.

As my inner ceremony of confirming my self-love drew to its end, I became distracted by an indigo light beaming into my third eye chakra. This hovering light was familiar; it was Bluebell, my fairy guide whom I had been aware of since my early childhood. I opened myself up to Bluebell's presence.

"Bluebell, I greet you with love and joy!"

Bluebell only appeared to me as an indigo orb of light. Sometimes I would glimpse the tiny features of her face or a hand. I knew she was light in the same way we are as humans, except she could show herself in any form she wished to. From a young age, I had chosen to perceive her as her truth, viewing the vibrancy of her light while experiencing the vibration of her energy as she communicated with me. Her words always entered my mind as if they were my own; they were projected from her soul as sound frequencies through my third eye chakra into my thoughts.

"Nara, I have been sent to you by Butterfly Moon to call on your assistance and support. There is great turmoil in the elemental kingdom on Atlantis, and we urgently need your help!"

Bluebell's energy was sharp and piercing as she communicated with me. Her normal gentle, serene, and childlike vibration was absent today.

"Tell me what is happening," I said while lovingly comforting her in my energy.

"The elemental kingdom is being suppressed. We are being forced to leave Earth and discard our roles within nature." Bluebell's energy vibration became more frantic, sounding like shrieks within my mind.

"The nature lands of Atlantis will not survive without beings such as yourself. You nurture and feed nature with light. If the elementals leave Earth, then the light and purity of the nature kingdom will be diminished! How can this happen?" Again, I demanded more information from Bluebell.

"We feel as if we are being suppressed by negativity. Messages have arrived from the central areas of Atlantis sharing information that much of the elemental kingdom already surrendered in those areas, returning through portals in nature to the inner planes for safety. We have been told a group of priestesses and priests have accessed energy from the stars that they are transmitting into a temple. These priests and priestesses are making machinery to dissolve separation between heaven and Earth, between the stars and Earth, and between human bodies and energetic bodies. They mean to bring the Creator into full manifestation on Earth through special technology. They have built a machine that reconfigures the energetic grids and magnetic structure of Earth.

"We, the elementals, have an energetic grid system within the planet that aids us to exist on Earth. The intentions of the priests and priestesses seem amicable, yet they are deactivating the elemental grid of Earth. I feel they do not recognize the implications of their actions. The elemental grid of Earth designed to sustain our energies is being destroyed as all the life force energy is sucked from the grid and our beings into the machine so that it can be used as power for further manifestations. To us, it feels as if the energetic structure and security of the world we know is falling away, as if the ground is disappearing from beneath us. If the elemental energetic gird of Earth is destroyed, there will be no anchor for our energies; our existence will be erased from Earth."

"I am aware that all beings — human, animal, elemental, and so forth — have a template and anchor built into an energetic grid embedded across the entire Earth. Each of the energetic grids is unique and holds tremendous volumes of life force energy. Akin to a magnetic grid, they hold our memories and sustain us within our realities," I thought out loud. "Through their machine, the priests and priestesses must be trying to manipulate the elemental grid without realizing they are deactivating it. Their work could cause elementals to become extinct, kill our beautiful nature lands, and even starve humans of food and life force energy. Bluebell, do you know what I can do to help you?" I waited patiently for her to answer. My mind was beginning to whirl with questions and scenarios.

"Butterfly Moon, our communicator on behalf of the fairies, has moved through the fairy portal to work on the inner planes. She shared her instructions with me. Please come with me to the fairy portal, and please call your friends to join us," Bluebell pleaded.

I began to scramble from my stone in the center of the river, but I caught myself and sat back down. I realized I could send a telepathic message to Benjamin, asking him to gather people and bring them to the fairy portal, which was in the woods close to my temple. Linking into Benjamin's energy, I visualized him standing before me and spoke all I needed to share with him as if we were having a conversation in my mind. His response took a moment, but then I felt his energy flow to me as his words entered my mind: "Nara, I hear you. I will be with you shortly." I felt Benjamin's love fill my senses.

I rose from the rock and waded through the cool water of the river to the green grassy bank. I paused for only a moment to dry my wet feet on the velvety grass before breaking into a run, gathering the length of my pale-pink dress into my arms as my stride lengthened. Bluebell hovered before me as if directing me to the fairy portal. I reached the pathway that veered around our community and rose diagonally upward to the left side of the woods that led to the temple. In no time, I had run along a weaving pathway edged with bushes, across an open expanse, and into the wooded area. I slowed down to negotiate the trees and to adjust to the uphill climb, finding a pathway of my own to my destination.

Benjamin entered my mind as I sensed his energy around me.

"I am traveling to you now," he shared. "I have a group of people with me."

"We are nearly there, Nara," Bluebell assured me.

My breathing was becoming heavy, and my body felt as if it wished to give way with the stress of my movements. I smiled and nodded to Bluebell, inhaling deeply.

I almost ran into the large amethyst crystal point that had been placed to mark the presence of the fairy portal. I slowed down, leaning over to regulate my breathing. Once I could raise my head, I observed my surroundings. I could see the circles of multicolored light emanating from the center of the portal. The tip of the amethyst crystal point was directly in line with the center of the portal, so it appeared as if the portal was protruding from its tip. Waves of light emanated into the woods, which meant the portal was strong and still open. I noticed many fairies hovering around the center of the portal, some quickly dashing into the portal's center and vanishing — only to return again. The overall atmosphere was of frustration and uncertainty.

"Many fairies in this area are moving toward the fairy portal for safety. There are numerous other portals within this area for other elemental beings, but some portals are already beginning to close. The fairies you see at the center of the portal, who move into the center and then return, are ensuring the portal remains open and strong," Bluebell explained.

I could hear footsteps weaving through the woods, and they became louder and louder until I was surrounded by a group of familiar faces who rushed into the space, some gasping for air. Benjamin was at my side instantly, his face and presence as serene as ever. I noticed that gratitude was always his expression and the energy he used to interact with his reality. Jayda was at my other side, and these two robust, tall men gave me an unexpected boost of strength. Leesha, Jayda's partner, smiled glowingly at me. Martyna and Parlo were present with

Hamna, Violet, and Amka. So many beautiful friends from our community gathered around me, creating an atmosphere of unconditional love and support. We were thirty or more gathered in the woods around the fairy portal.

I began to explain the situation to my friends and family, sharing all the information Bluebell had provided. The energy of determination grew in the group as many people questioned how they could be of service. I turned to Bluebell, waiting for her guidance, and then relayed her words: "Please help us to reactivate the elemental grids of Earth and to counteract the destruction being caused."

"Nara, I have an idea." Benjamin said. "Do you remember Jacoree, the tree who has anchored the vibration, light, and consciousness of the Celestial White Beings? I have this inspiration that through Jacoree, we could awaken all the trees in Atlantis, sending the energy of the Celestial White Beings through the trees' energetic grid while holding an intention of the light overflowing and penetrating the elemental energetic grid, causing their grid to be purified and reactivated in all areas of Atlantis. The energy of the Celestial White Beings would be able to anchor through the trees and bring healing, raising the vibration of Atlantis as well." Benjamin then fell silent, allowing everyone to process his words. Almost instantly, everyone began to shout out in agreement.

"Nara?" Benjamin gazed into my eyes looking for acceptance and approval.

With Bluebell beaming love and confirmation at me, I nodded my head in agreement.

"Benjamin, I will stay here with the fairy portal. Will you take everyone to Jacoree and begin the activation?"

Benjamin leaned forward to kiss me on my forehead before turning sharply to lead the way. Jacoree was positioned almost in line with the fairy portal on the northeast side above our community, so Benjamin broke into a run to reach the tree as quickly as possible. I watched them all leave, and it looked as if they were being swallowed by the surrounding woods.

I felt a sense of loneliness as I was left in solitude once more. I realized my greatest enjoyment was to be surrounded by my loved ones and friends — to see, sense, and acknowledge the divine spark of the Creator within each and experience interactions of love. Letting go of the loneliness trying to linger in my heart, I turned my attention to Bluebell.

"How can I be of service?"

"Nara, please sit before the fairy portal. Make a connection with all fairies, and allow yourself to hold the fairy portal open on behalf of the fairies."

"This is all you ask of me?" I questioned, somewhat in disbelief.

"For now," Bluebell responded.

Sitting down comfortably, I gazed into the portal and called on the Celestial White Beings to channel through my being and into the portal. At once, white light flashed through my body, surging into the earth and expressing from my heart chakra into the center of the portal, which began to expand its energy field, intensifying its light. I could feel myself becoming a portal of light and merging with the fairy portal.

"Good, Nara. Now connect with Benjamin," Bluebell encouraged.

Without a thought or an intention, I was given an image of Benjamin. He had now reached Jacoree. The entire group was standing in amazement as Benjamin called on the Celestial White Beings' energy to channel through Jacoree.

The trunk of the tree pulsated with brilliant, glistening white light. The light shimmered as it flowed into the branches and leaves, creating an aura of white light around the tree and extending into the earth. I could see each person's face lit by the radiance Jacoree was emanating.

Benjamin quickly turned to face the group and asked them to find a tree they felt drawn to in the surrounding area and work with the spirit of the tree to draw the energy and consciousness of the Celestial White Beings into its being, replicating Jacoree. Benjamin remembered his first union with Jacoree and encouraged the group to find trees that wished to be of service, reminding them that everything has the ability to merge in oneness and completeness with the Creator.

I watched as the group scattered, communicating with the trees around them. I saw that some people instantly found trees willing to be of service while others required a few attempts of communication to identify willing trees. After a few moments, I saw glimmers of light flashing through several tree trunks, and gradually pure white light filled several, entering their roots, branches, and leaves. The trees were joyfully bathing in the celestial vibrations.

Bluebell woke me from my vision, putting me to work.

"Nara, focus the light you are channeling into the elemental grid system of Earth."

Allowing the light of the Celestial White Beings to flow from my heart into the portal, I focused my attention on the energy already flowing into the earth. I directed it with my thoughts to the elemental grid system of Earth. I had no idea what the grid would look like or where it might be positioned in relation to me; I simply imagined the pure white light flowing from my being as a river of liquid light entering the earth. I held a strong intention of the light reaching the elemental grid system, bathing, restoring, and activating it once more. I imagined light surging across all of Atlantis.

Visions of Benjamin and our group came flooding into my mind. The group was asking the trees to connect with other trees and transmit the light to all trees across Atlantis. Large areas of trees came alight with pure white light. Like a bird soaring in the sky, I could see the land of Atlantis to the south looking as if a fire were spreading as every tree became a radiant beacon of light. White light shone into the land and sky. Never before had I seen such a magnitude of magnificent and brilliant white light on Earth! It was extremely beautiful and impressive. Each tree responded to our plea, to our intention, and accepted the light of the Celestial White Beings.

With the light so present on Earth, I felt the group's fervent intention as one penetrating voice that encouraged the trees to share the vibrant light they had received and distribute it into the elemental grid system. The light emanating from the trees diminished slightly as they began to work with the elemental grid system of Earth. I could feel everyone inhaling deeply as if waiting in anticipation for a response from the grid that would confirm our valiant efforts were working. I could sense eagerness and hope building within my being as we waited in silence.

My attention instantly snapped back to the portal before me as if drawn by a magnet. I opened my eyes to see hundreds of fairies of all different colors of light flying back through the portal. They were bombarding me, and more and more fairies propelled themselves back through the portal. I was surrounded by orbs of light glistening, beaming, and hovering around me.

"The fairies have returned!" I shouted in jubilation. My cry transmitted to the group and confirmed the work we had achieved. The gathered fairies gradually dispersed, and this welcomed more fairies from the inner planes back to Earth.

"Nara, the elemental grid has been reactivated. The fairies can now anchor their energies back into Earth and continue their purpose. I wish you to know that the light you and your friends channeled from the Celestial White Beings and the support of the tree spirits also transmitted into the central temples. The power of your combined light melted the machine that was deactivating the elemental grid. Nara, on behalf of the fairies, I thank you for reacting to our plea." Bluebell shared her gratitude with me openly as she hovered before my third eye, penetrating my mind with her indigo light.

"I am always here for you — all of you. I love you so much," I shared with Bluebell.

I waited for as long as felt appropriate — until the portal felt strong enough to remain open and the last of the fairies moved through it. I then gathered myself and slowly began to walk to Jacoree, believing I might find the others waiting.

I wandered somewhat wearily through the trees, marveling at what had been achieved — how we had reactivated the elemental grid to save the nature kingdom and the elementals from suffering. Everything had occurred so quickly, yet we had been guided and supported within every moment. I felt a great envelopment of being loved and blessed in so many ways. I was so enthralled in my thoughts and memories that I nearly walked straight into Benjamin.

"Nara, I was walking to find you. I thought you might still be at the fairy portal," Benjamin said, placing his arms around my waist.

"Congratulations! I saw all you were doing with the group and the trees. It was so beautiful. It is amazing to imagine we made a difference. My work with the fairies is complete now, so I thought I would come and find you and the others," I shared with excitement, my heart bubbling with love for Benjamin. Our telepathic connection, how we had worked as one, reinforced my belief in the Creator in bringing us together to support each other and Atlantis. Benjamin gently and lovingly guided me in the direction of Jacoree.

"I thought we could sit for a while together with Jacoree to rest and oversee the energy transmissions taking place," Benjamin offered as we reached the tree.

He encouraged me to sit down with my back against Jacoree's trunk. I instantly felt the tree's presence ground and balance my energies. I had not realized I had experienced such high vibrations and needed to connect once more into the earth to embody the energies within my physical body, encouraging me to be consciously present. I looked with renewed energies deeply into Benjamin's eyes.

"You're back!" he exclaimed.

Benjamin drew my body close into his. The touch of his skin against mine, the warmth of his body, and the strength in his arms caused a deep vibration of love to erupt from within me, filling my every sense with an overwhelming experience of ecstasy and pleasure. Lifting my face up to his with his loving hand, he kissed me. My senses were already reeling, and my energy melted deeply into his as if our auras, bodies, and souls had merged to become one. Peace, bliss, and a love that felt divine washed over us as we were elevated into the heavens of the Creator, into the supreme and vibrant light of the Creator. And so I relaxed deeper, with consent and contentment for the divine plan unfolding for our souls on Atlantis emanating from every cell of my being.

Nara's Notes

The greatest power you hold and embody is your power of unconditional love. It is your strength, your gift, and your tool for creating your reality. Everything is born from love, and everything returns to love; there is no escaping love. When you accept yourself as a loving being, recognizing this to be your natural eternal existence, you empower yourself with strength and the ability to experience a divine reality on Earth. All frustrations, pains, and suffering simply fall away, no longer holding the power over you that they once did. When you learn to love yourself unconditionally, you prepare yourself to be loved by others unconditionally, offering yourself the freedom to be powerful and to share your love vibration openly and easily. When you purify yourself and accept the love of the Creator around and within you, you naturally step into a state of empowerment. You cannot help becoming and expressing your true self. When you fail to prioritize love, you hide yourself from the world and your loved ones, creating a false identity and reality for yourself.

Through our experience of supporting the elemental kingdom and the fairies, Benjamin and I accessed our inner power and realized we could make a difference in our realities, facilitating shifts and healing in the realities of others when they are willing and accepting. You are not powerless in your reality; you are powerful and can make divinely guided and supported shifts for yourself and others.

Your Atlantean soul can demonstrate many qualities of your soul to you — your power, your qualities of love, and your qualities of lack of love. Therefore, it is important to connect with your Atlantean self and begin to form a relationship of connection to aid deep healing and transformation within your current reality and your Atlantean reality.

Practice 18
Establish a Fairy Connection

The intention of this meditation is to support you in connecting with the fairy kingdom and your fairy guide. Say out loud or in your mind,

I call on Fairy Bluebell to draw close into my auric field and to

support me in being surrounded by the energy and presence of the fairy kingdom, experiencing their beautiful and vibrant light shining lovingly around me. I now choose to inhale the light of the fairy kingdom to build a connection with the fairies.

Imagine, sense, or acknowledge Bluebell's indigo light before your third eye chakra. Breathe the indigo light into your third eye chakra, and notice as the fairy kingdom surrounds you in their multicolor light. Know through focus on your breath that you are connecting with the fairy kingdom.

Bluebell, I ask that if you have any guidance or inspiration appropriate to share with me, please support me in receiving it clearly now. I also wish to connect with my own fairy guide(s), so please bring my fairy guide(s) forth to me for my acknowledgment and acceptance. Thank you.

Be receptive. You may receive guidance, inspiration, symbols, or visions from Bluebell. She might also bring forth your fairy guide. You can ask for a name, the color, or any details you wish to know about your fairy guide. Allow yourself to have patience and faith in your abilities to receive.

Practice 19
Heal with the Fairies

By experiencing and inhaling the presence of the fairies, you can call on their healing energy to flow into your being. Take as long as you wish to allow the fairies to heal you. Your soul also has its own powerful healing vibration, which you can access with intention. By merging the healing vibrations of the fairies and your soul within your heart chakra, you can imagine the healing energy as a wave of light flowing from your heart chakra into Earth, connecting with all the energetic grids of the planet. Especially imagine or hold focus on your healing light flowing into the elemental grid system of Earth, bringing life and the light of the Creator to the elementals, the nature kingdom, humanity, and the planet as an entire being.

Practice 20
Accept Your Atlantean Self

You have the ability to view, connect, and communicate with your Atlantean self; this is the purpose of this exercise. It might take time and patience as you allow yourself to open up to receive the presence of an aspect of your self and soul. It is important to dissolve all doubts and trust in any insights that may come forth to you. Say out loud,

I now invoke the angels of Atlantis and Nara Merlyn to draw close into my auric field, surrounding me completely in the energy and vibration of love. I ask you to transport me to the Celestial White Beings' temple on the northern side of Atlantis so that I may begin to reconnect or become aware of my own Atlantean energies. Thank you.

Imagine, sense, or acknowledge yourself sitting in my temple surrounded by the pure white light of the Celestial White Beings. Say out loud,

I now invoke my Atlantean self to step forth and exist before me.

Imagine or hold the focus of sending the love of your heart into your Atlantean self as he or she exists before you. Your light now flows into your Atlantean self's heart chakra and returns to you, creating a figure eight — the symbol of infinity — between you as your heart and love energy link.

You may have had several Atlantean lifetimes, as there were three different Atlantean civilizations. There isn't a need to discover all your Atlantean lifetimes; the most appropriate one will step forth to be acknowledged. You may call on my energy (Nara) to support you in connecting with and gaining understanding of your Atlantean self.

Below are questions you can ask your Atlantean self to deepen your connection and understanding. Ask one question at a time, sitting in acceptance of any form of answer that might flow forth. If an answer doesn't flow, remember to love yourself unconditionally, and try another question. Know the answers and inspiration will flow with divine timing.

- *Is my Atlantean self male or female?*
- *How old is my Atlantean self that comes forth to me now?*
- *What is the name of my Atlantean self?*
- *Did my Atlantean self visit the Celestial White Beings' temple?*
- *What is the appearance of my Atlantean self?*

When you feel the process and connection are completed and you wish to return to your physical reality, invite the angels of Atlantis to ground your energies and any healing that may have taken place back in your physical reality on Earth. Imagine with each exhale that light and energy flow from your body through your feet and into Mother Earth. Say out loud,

I am grounded, centered, balanced, and ready to continue my blissful reality on Earth.

CHAPTER

10

The Blessing

After a few days of preparations, the time arrived for Benjamin's and my blessing. Many people in our community had experienced blessings from the Celestial White Beings and were guided, through me, to bring truth and a public display of their devotion and love for each other. Often couples wished to demonstrate their love for each other before the Creator, to be blessed by the universe and the sacred energies of the Creator to allow the divine will of their partnership to embed into their beings and reality. A blessing in my temple was always something I found heart expanding; the atmosphere and vibration of love seemed to be enhanced within all present, hanging in the air for days after. I was also aware that the blessings and ceremonies seemed to lift the love vibration of our entire community as if the couple were anchoring a sacred chamber of the Creator's love with their united love, which gathered us all in its vibration.

Benjamin and I had spent the night in the temple in complete meditation and communion with the Celestial White Beings. We had not slept, yet we felt more alive and replenished than ever before. We sat at opposite sides of the temple, our backs resting against the curved walls. Breathing deeply as the last rays of sunlight faded, we entered a state of peace and conscious awareness, calling on the Celestial White Beings' presence to work with our energies and prepare us for the blessing — which would occur just after dawn the following day.

We didn't commune with each other but worked individually with the Celestial White Beings to access and draw celestial templates, codes, energetic patterns, wisdom, and consciousness into our beings. I cannot remember my experiences or even the wisdom shared; however, I do remember my soul expanding as if it were an intense, hot liquid light, penetrating my body and filling me with loving warmth. I remember feeling as if much of myself, my personality and identity, were falling away — so much so there was a period when I felt as if I had lost myself only to discover the magnificence within my being with a tremendous familiarity. The energy of the Celestial White Beings was my constant companion, continually vivid in my awareness.

Standing now in my temple with all my loved ones surrounding me, Benjamin strongly grounded next to me, and Hamna before me — his smile beaming on us — I felt as if I had been reborn, as if I was a new person able to experience and conceive only love. I noticed the most beautiful dance of love playing out energetically among us all as we gathered with the Celestial White Beings to experience the love chamber of the Creator. Blessings of bliss and truth cascaded from the divine onto our heads and into hearts.

In my hands, I held a bouquet of pink flowers my mother and father had gifted to me, symbolizing their eternal and unconditional love for me. The beauty of the flowers was overwhelming; it was not their physical presence but the love they carried from my parents that penetrated deep into my heart. My simple gown was pure white, symbolizing my divinity and my surrender to be as one with the Creator.

Benjamin stood next to me in a pure white tunic, his blue eyes glistening with delight and gratitude. It felt to me as if he was riding a wave of complete divine love that just kept rising and accelerating with no reason to stop. Benjamin held a bunch of white flowers gifted to him by Amka, his most recent spiritual mentor. Benjamin's parents had given him to their local temple to become a devotee to the Creator when he was nine years old, and he had not seen them since. He didn't even know their whereabouts in Atlantis. This had not bothered him, as the note his parents had left with him at that young age shared that they felt he was born as a son of the Creator and so they gave him to the Creator to be of service. The white flowers Benjamin held seemed to emanate his loving service to all souls and aspects of the Creator. I felt extremely proud to be standing next to him and excited by the prospect of receiving a blessing.

Everyone around me was dressed in the most beautiful colors, ranging from vibrant to pale pastel. The energy they exuded was a feeling of being thrilled and energized as they began to tone the word "Om," the sacred sound of the universe. The echoes of voices flew through the temple and cascaded down on Benjamin and me. The blessing had begun.

Hamna then spoke with great pride, reassurance, and knowingness.

"We have congregated here today in this sacred temple to bear witness to the divine connection, union, and love Nara and Benjamin share for each other, guided and encouraged by the divine will of the Creator. We recognize them as two of the same soul group and a physical manifestation of the Celestial White Beings. We collect our attention, focus, and consciousness to witness the love and union between them while celebrating the love of the Creator within Nara, Benjamin, and us all. Nara and Benjamin hold the intention of joining their energies and souls as one to experience the spiritual growth this can bring while respecting their divine purpose together in this era on Atlantis. As a community and a collective, we trust in the love Nara and Benjamin hold for each other and the divine will of the Creator, which blesses this sacred union. As the masculine and feminine vibrations of the Creator become balanced within Nara and Benjamin and within their relationship, we recognize the same shift of harmony within our own beings. Knowing within our hearts that the Celestial White Beings and the Creator have prepared them for their future together, we collectively give our support for the merging of their love, light, and souls at all appropriate levels of their beings."

Hamna nodded in acknowledgment, as if personally addressing everyone in the temple, as pure love and happiness billowed from his heart. His face then altered as his energies shifted into another dimension. He traveled quickly into a deep-seated peace, preparing himself to welcome the words of the Celestial White Beings for this celebratory occasion. The mist of the Celestial White Beings began to settle around us, embracing us in love.

"Beloved Nara and Benjamin, we are the Celestial White Beings. We wish to guide you now in your sacred blessing ceremony. Please join your hands together in union."

Hamna spoke clearly and loudly the words of the Celestial White Beings. He reached gently for our hands. With Benjamin's left palm chakra facing the sky, Hamna placed my right hand on top so that our palm chakras met.

"Please close your eyes, taking the attention of your minds into your heart chakras and into the very seat of your souls. Let your attention penetrate the Celestial White Beings' vibrations of your souls as you become encapsulated and bathed in light. Permit your souls to spiral from your hearts into the heavens to connect with the core of the Creator's vibration. As your individual souls spiral, they merge, becoming one spiral and connection. Welcome the soul aspect of your partner into your soul, instigating a deeply contented state of completion within you. Feel your souls merge inside your being." The Celestial White Beings paused.

Expansion, exhilaration, and a deeper love than I had ever experienced pulsated through my being, and I felt the familiar energy of Benjamin embrace me completely. It was welcomed within the deepest, most personal space within my soul, which I could only just comprehend. It felt as if the universe was melding together in harmony as thousands of angels drew intimately close to share their blessings of love with us. Our energy spiraled as one with greater intensity into the core of the Creator as the blessings of the Creator showered down on us with concentrated strength. It felt as if the universe was rejoicing by sharing gifts of light, love, illumination, and insights with us all.

I could hear people exclaim with joy as they also experienced the downpour of light. I was reminded of the words Martyna had read from the scroll that stated when Benjamin and I merged together, it would symbolize to the universe that help was required on Atlantis to maintain its high vibration. With energy beating down on us, it truly felt as if the universe was responding by sending streams of light into the energetic foundations of Atlantis as well as emanating them from the crystals of the temple across the land.

Hamna again spoke the loving consciousness of the Celestial White Beings. "We, the Celestial White Beings, will now activate your divine plan within your beings. This has now altered, due to your union, so your divine plan for your souls and Earth holds the vibration of oneness. This activation is akin to a fire igniting within you and guiding you both forth as one."

Fire of white, gold, pink, and blue burst into activity within my being as love exploded from me with such depth to each person present from our community. A bond was being formed as Benjamin and I delivered the love consciousness and template of the Creator to all, reawakening all to love. While the love felt beyond and larger than me, all I could do was smile with glee.

"Nara and Benjamin, we need not present you with any physical representation of your love and devotion for each other nor share with you a symbol of your unity; however, we choose to return to you a tool of magnification. We give to you now the Celestial White Beacons to aid your journey and mission together on Earth. It is with this gift we shower you in our blessings, knowing the ceremony is now complete. We give our loving blessings and consent to your union."

With the completion of the communication from the Celestial White Beings, Hamna grounded himself and drew his presence to be with us once more.

I remained in a state of expansion until the energies around and within me settled and filtered into my physical body, allowing me to become aware of my hand being tightly grasped and supported by Benjamin's loving hand. I opened my eyes to experience the temple filled with beautiful radiant sunlight and many smiling faces focused on us. Benjamin, still holding my hand, gently pulled me into an embrace with his right arm wrapping comfortingly around me. As our bodies touched, an electrifying energy soared up my spine and filled my mind with a peaceful ecstasy.

"I love you with all my essence," Benjamin shared, gazing into my eyes and then kissing me with confirmation. The love we were creating for each other surrounded us like a cocoon. Benjamin's words weren't needed, yet they materialized our experience and new existence.

"The Celestial White Beings mentioned the return of the Celestial White Beacons. What do you think they meant?" I whispered to Benjamin to retain our private space.

Drawing his mouth close to my left ear, he whispered, "In meditation, I have been inspired by the appearance of two identical pure white crystal wands with a point at one end. These crystal wands have been swimming in my mind for some time. They are tools from the Celestial White Beings, and they have the power to magnify anything we wish to manifest. They are powerful, Nara, and will serve us well in our journey together."

Benjamin looked down to our hands still clasped tightly. Lifting my hand gently, I saw in Benjamin's palm the wands he had just described. They were beautiful and held a high and pure celestial vibration.

I gently grasped the White Beacon that most attracted my attention, claiming it as my own. Benjamin smiled down at me in agreement.

"You know, we are the Celestial White Beacons of Atlantis. This is the message from the Celestial White Beings, and we can encourage many more people to be beacons to save Atlantis," he said.

Both Benjamin and I carefully concealed our white beacons in pockets in our garments as people gathered around us, wishing to embrace and congratulate us on our blessing and union. Everyone seemed to buzz with love, wishing to give and receive love in this most sacred moment.

Hamna gathered Benjamin and me into his arms and said, "So your journey together begins, and the survival of Atlantis rests with you and us all. Keep those White Beacons safe; they are treasures of the universe, given to many civilizations by the Celestial White Beings at times of crisis. Nara, Benjamin, we know we are truly blessed with the arrival of the Celestial White Beacons. Keep them with you and safe always," Hamna warned.

A loud rhythmic drumbeat traveled through the temple, attracting everyone's attention. A second and third drumbeat soon joined the first, creating an exhilarating sound that captured the essence and power of love in the temple. My father led the sound, walking into the center of the temple with his drum. The other drummers followed, and Parlo encouraged everyone to dance.

Parlo shouted with joy, sharing his heart and inner guidance with all. "Send the love we have received and activated into the earth through joyous dancing and stamping your feet. Let Mother Earth and all of humanity receive the love we have and feel its rhythm. Let us create a new rhythmic pattern of love for Earth and humanity in deep celebration and grounding of Nara and Benjamin's devoted love to each other and us all."

We couldn't resist following Parlo's guidance; his heart was singing for us to do so. Everyone jumped into action, dancing, jumping, spinning, and stamping their feet in the ecstasy of love. Benjamin kept me close to him, wanting to share every moment with me. We danced and screamed in exhilaration as our love flowed deep into Mother Earth's energetic body and physical form. She was drawing close to us, receiving in gratitude all we wished to share. We were all in a state of heaven and celebration of our truth.

After some time, Martyna and Amka brought refreshments — delicious fruits and pure spring water — into the temple, distributing them to everyone present to rejuvenate our physical bodies. Benjamin and I collapsed in a state of relief and liberation. His back rested up against the temple wall, and I was completely immersed and integrated in his energy as I rested my back against his strong chest, my head nestled into his neck. I felt only bliss. The dancing had helped to ground us all, allowing our bodies, emotions, and minds to process the light we had received.

Jayda collected the crystal singing bowls he had once given to me into the center of the temple and began to play a hypnotically beautiful sound, which enhanced our state of peace and liberation. Everyone sat down with loved ones to receive Jayda's sound healing.

Benjamin and I spent the rest of our day with our loved ones celebrating and sharing the love in our hearts. It was truly a love-inspiring experience. My heart burst with each moment; my reunion with Benjamin made me feel as if I had reached heaven and would be fulfilled forevermore. I knew we would always be together, for these were the vows we made to each other.

Nara's Notes

Blessings from the universe, the Creator, our souls, or the Celestial White Beings do not have to be for special occasions only. Each and every day or moment of your reality, you can ask for a blessing. It is most likely that you will receive a boost or download of much-needed or appropriate energy into your being. A blessing can confirm, magnify, support, or even manifest situations into your reality that the Divine believes to be appropriate for your journey. Such blessings are symbols of the sacred universe honoring you as you recognize you are worthy of attention and support.

You can invite your guides, soul, soul group, and the Creator to shower you in divine and appropriate blessings each morning when you awaken. This symbolizes that you are instantly attuned to the Creator, open to and welcoming the divine abundance and assistance of the Creator in your being and reality. It is also a beautiful practice to bless all manifestations within your reality or that you receive. Blessings of this nature can be simple expressions of gratitude, welcoming, happiness, and trust.

The Creator is always ready to divinely intervene, support you, guide you, and solve all problems or disharmony. We often forget to invite the Creator to do so, or sometimes we are too attached to a circumstance that doesn't serve us. When we invite the Creator into our being and reality, we open ourselves to receive, which is a powerful state and can allow for miraculous beneficial situations to manifest. Any form of blessing is a welcome invitation to the Creator to become divinely manifested in greater ways than we have previously experienced.

Benjamin and I received a blessing for our union so that we could make the most of our connection and ensure that our relationship would be eternally guided by the Creator aspects within us. We invited the Creator to be a part of our reality; or more correctly, we recognized the Creator as a part of our reality and being. It is important to remember that although we invite the Creator to be with us, we are actually recognizing that the Creator has always been permanently present.

Practice 21
Soul Mate Connections

Many lightworkers wish to connect with or experience a reality with their soul mates. A life focused on ascension can be a lonely experience, so to have someone beside you who understands you like no other can be a powerful desire. A soul mate is often someone from your soul group or sometimes a soul not from your soul group whom you have connected with in multiple lifetimes — someone you have experienced a deep bond with. Many people want to experience their soul mates because they desire to be loved unconditionally and completely. This desire for a soul mate is often a stage of ascension. A realization dawns that the Creator is the only source who can truly nurture and love you completely and with whom you can feel a deep oneness. This realization opens you up, encouraging you to love yourself unconditionally. The more you love yourself unconditionally, the more you attract your soul mate or a person into your reality to exist in harmony with you, whether it is in a romantic way or as a deep friendship of understanding and connection.

Often people are not ready to recognize their soul mates — of which they might have many. It is only when they love themselves that they realize they are divinely worthy of such a connection. A soul mate connection offers a deeply nurturing experience, and it can also manifest as a mirror so that you see yourself in the other person. Your love and your negative habits may be portrayed to you by your soul mate, which can be difficult and requires strength, depending on the circumstances.

Whether you are in a relationship or have supportive spiritual friends — or not — you can connect with your soul mate's energy in existence on the inner planes. Some of our soul mates choose to support us from the inner planes and do not incarnate on Earth, while others are present on Earth. Connecting in meditation with your soul mates on the inner planes can bring feelings of comfort, support, and contentment to your soul as the connection fuels inner love for yourself. Wisdom and necessary information can also be shared through the connection. Soul mates on Earth can also be attracted to you if it is divinely appropriate. If you are in a loving relationship and connect with soul mate energy on the inner planes, it will not cause the Earth relationship to cease — unless that is the will of the Creator. The purpose of the practice I wish to share with you is to dissolve the yearning for a connection with your soul mates and to bring forth healing and contentment whether your soul mates are present or not.

Allow yourself to enter a state of meditation, peace, and stillness. Then say out loud,

I call on my beloved guides, soul, and soul group to oversee my process of soul integration. I acknowledge and know deep within my being that I am loved unconditionally by all aspects of the Creator. I acknowledge and know that I love myself unconditionally and accept myself completely.

In a space of love and truth within and around me, I call on my soul mate or soul mates to draw close and connect with me if it is divinely appropriate. Let me feel the love we hold for each other and the bond of our souls. My purpose for our connection is to bring only healing and contentment to my soul so that I know I am as one and in loving connection with my soul mates, whether they are on Earth or the inner planes. [Optional: Through my connection today, my intention is to call forth, with divine timing, a soul mate relationship or friendship into physical manifestation on Earth with me so that I may experience a deeply loving bond with an aspect of myself and the Creator in this lifetime. Thank you.] Assist me in becoming aware of the loving energy and any inspiration I need to understand through connection with my soul mate. Thank you.

Let yourself breathe in the energy surrounding you. A being or energy may make itself known to you; a memory or energy may dawn from within you. Let yourself give space for exploration, trusting in your senses.

When you have completed the process, there is no need to disconnect yourself. Simply ask your soul mate to step back and allow you to be free from any unneeded influences.

If you seek a romantic relationship, then by calling forth the soul mate who has the divine potential to exist with you on Earth, you can allow yourself to become familiar with the soul mate's energy so that when you meet on Earth, there will be instant recognition and familiarity.

Practice 22
Recall Atlantean Relationships

My purpose is to support you in discovering your Atlantean journey, so in this practice, I encourage you to connect on a deeper level with the Atlantean self you previously linked with. Say out loud,

I now invoke the angels of Atlantis and Nara Merlyn to draw close into my auric field, completely surrounding me in the energy and vibration of love. I ask you to transport me to the Celestial White Beings' temple on the northern side of Atlantis so that I may continue to reconnect or become aware of my own Atlantean energies. Thank you."

Imagine, sense, or acknowledge yourself sitting in my temple surrounded by the pure white light of the Celestial White Beings. Say out loud,

I now invoke my Atlantean self to step forth and exist before me.

Imagine or hold the focus as you send the love of your heart into your Atlantean self as he or she exists. Your light flows into your Atlantean self's heart chakra and returns to you, creating a figure eight, the symbol of infinity, between you as your heart and love energy link.

Below are questions you can ask your Atlantean self to deepen your connection and understanding. Say out loud,

- *Inspire, describe, or allow me to remember the position or role of my Atlantean self in Nara's community or any other community on Atlantis.*
- *Assist me in remembering whether my Atlantean self had a loving romantic relationship, was single, or experienced some thing else. Show me where my Atlantean self directed his or her love.*
- *Did my Atlantean self exist in a family? Did I have brothers, sisters, or maybe beloved friends?*

After a period of exploration that follows your inner guidance, inspiration, or feelings, focus on bringing healing to all forms of relationships your Atlantean self was involved in. Say out loud,

With the pure, healing, overflowing love of the Creator penetrating my being and flowing in all directions into my heart center, I exist now as an instrument of love and healing. I emanate my love and healing into the representation of my Atlantean self before me and, more importantly, into the aspect of my Atlantean self within me. My purpose is to heal all wounds, scars, pains, suffering, and other forms of unneeded energy that may have been caused by the relationships my Atlantean self formed and his or her actions within those relationships. If any of this unneeded energy is projecting into my current lifetime and behavior, I now ask for and initiate a complete cleansing and purification process on all levels of my being, eternally dissolving this unneeded energy.

Breathe deeply and experience the healing and loving vibrations the Creator shares with you, knowing you are melting away all unneeded energies with every breath you exhale.

When you feel the process and connection has come to completion and you wish to return to your physical reality, simply invite the angels of Atlantis to ground your energies and any healing that may have taken place back in your physical reality on Earth. With each exhalation, imagine light and energy flowing from your body through your feet and into Mother Earth.

I am grounded, centered, balanced, and ready to continue my blissful reality on Earth.

CHAPTER

11

The Warning

The blessing for Benjamin and me had been a beautiful, high-vibrational, and joy-filled day, yet several days passed afterward when it felt as though the energy vibration on Atlantis had fallen somewhat. The vibrations we all experienced at the blessing had made our souls soar, but the atmosphere the next day was a harmful mood of negativity, depletion, and frustration. It was something we had not expected in our community, as normally the love transmitted during a blessing carried us forward in a dance of love for quite a long period. Irritation and bad feelings within the community created a depression, which had never been seen before. Although Benjamin and I didn't feel annoyed by each other, we felt heaviness in the atmosphere weighing down on our community.

We decided to take matters into our own hands by encouraging the entire community to gather in the temple to ask the Celestial White Beings and the Creator for guidance, information, and healing. Such negative clouds within our beings previously had been unknown to us, but we knew if we did not take action, the negativity would project and manifest within the everyday realities and experiences.

Our community was a deeply connected group, which meant we had the power to manifest many things — especially when we were united in intention and focus. Some members of our community resisted coming to the temple, as they claimed they had more pressing matters, did not feel well, and even felt betrayed by the Celestial White Beings, though they could not explain why. These all seemed like false excuses created by the ego and fear.

After mentally sending the community a final clear message that shared our intention to gather, Benjamin and I surrendered, making our way to the temple to wait for anyone who chose to join us. On entering, we were reminded of the happiness of our blessing. Reaching out to each other, we embraced to share our happiness of being together in unison. Our energies merged as we lifted each other into quicker vibrations of light, feeling fear and negativity crumble away through the simple act of embracing. We looked into each other's eyes and chose to see divine love smiling back at us. We enjoyed our moments alone because we still hadn't had much time to really get to know each other on a physical or personality level, and being present with each other felt like a blessing from above, which we honored.

"Benjamin," I said tentatively, my voice echoing in the silent temple, "I don't know how to say this or even why it is coming into my emotions and feelings with such force and urgency, but I feel the need for us to bring forth a child of the light. I feel the soul is with us already. I have felt her energies around me even before our blessing. She has a powerful mission and purpose on Atlantis and is eager to be present with us. I had not before thought of bringing a child into this world; when one devotes themselves to the Creator, one does not think of such things. I know now you are a divine being of light, as am I. We are the Creator, and we have the divine right to manifest the Creator on Earth. It is a union, a creation, a validation of all we are. Every cell in my body is reaching for this new soul, wanting to merge with her by bringing our combined energies and souls as Nara and Benjamin together to create her in loving oneness. A child of oneness is to be born to help heal and inspire this reality, anchoring all her celestial light into Earth."

I gazed down at my feet, bashful and awkward. I had said all I felt — and more than I had wanted to.

Benjamin took my head in his loving hands and raised it so that my eyes met his once more. His gaze was concentrated and pure, filled with refined grace — as if he understood everything.

"She is a soul born from the Celestial White Beings. She is deeply loved and received by me and all," he said, and my entire body trembled with relief, gratitude, and acceptance.

"Do not fear, Nara. All is well. We are walking a guided pathway. We have not yet connected with each other intimately to honor our sacred sexual energies and powers; it is an adventure of discovery that will lead to a gift of bliss. Nara, the seed of creation planted within your being by the Celestial White Beings will be shared and gifted to her so that it continues to gradually integrate into the DNA of humanity."

Benjamin's reassurance connected us again on a deep level. Not only were we in tune with each other's loving vibrations, but we also recognized each other's fears, bringing only support rather than judgment.

"That is her name — isn't it? — Bliss," I said mischievously, as if we were both privy to the most amazing secret.

"Yes. She has come to me too, baring her soul to me. I know her in the same way you know her. She doesn't belong to us, and yet she will be born to us." Benjamin's eyes twinkled with joy and amusement. We jumped around like children, expressing sheer delight.

The central crystal in the ceiling began to vibrate as a white mist-like energy swirled into the temple. The door opened, and people began to flood in and make themselves comfortable on the temple floor. Benjamin and I were no longer alone, instead surrounded by many of the members of our community and the Celestial White Beings, all gazing expectantly at us. We realized our intention of gathering our community in the temple had manifested quicker than we had anticipated.

Benjamin and I sat down exactly where we stood — in the center of the temple. Holding hands, we breathed deeply to center our energies and connect to our souls through our heart chakras, like a gateway. We quickly moved into a space of peace together as if we were walking side by side. Our hearts beat as one, our breath followed a united rhythm, and our energy merged as if we were entering a well of light. The Celestial White Beings entered our energy and bodies and began to speak their words through us, which Benjamin and I shared simultaneously. The message was given forth through us with immense power, and no one could deny the presence of the Celestial White Beings working with us in the temple.

"Beloved souls of Atlantis, we honor and love you as you exist presently on Earth. Through Nara and Benjamin we have called you to be present with us so that we can share with you the vibration of freedom, thus returning you to your natural states of existence of happiness and joy. It is time for us to share truth with you, which is your divine right to understand."

Our voices harmoniously reverberated throughout the temple. I couldn't hear Benjamin's voice or my own clearly; instead, a new sound manifested from our united voices. There was a stirring in the temple as everyone readied themselves to receive the truth of the Celestial White Beings.

"For some time, your community has been a beacon of light on Atlantis, maintaining the vibration Atlanteans are accustomed to. Due to the presence of our temple, your community has also acted as a portal to bring forth energized light and wisdom from the inner planes to be embedded within Earth. The space you inhabit on Atlantis is deeply healing, and many across Atlantis know and understand this to be true. There are a number of communities on Atlantis that have a purpose such as yours — to sustain the light vibration of Atlantis for all — however, the central temples of Atlantis are growing in power. Their influence is manifesting intensely within the physical planes.

"You are all courageous souls. Your souls understand all that is occurring and the purpose and role of your presence at this time. We affirm to you now that you can trust in your soul, and you can trust in the power of love and light. Please refrain from accepting fear and negativity, because you know your hearts are more expansive and are able to be of service when you focus solely on love."

Gentle sounds of agreement filled the atmosphere of the temple as our friends and family enthusiastically resonated with the consciousness shared by the Celestial White Beings. I could feel the energy in the temple rising in frequency, and I knew we were all healing and letting go of fear from the simple supportive presence of the Celestial White Beings. Benjamin and I experienced the pure white light of our soul group building within us once more as our harmonious, blended voice echoed into the hearts of all present.

"The blessing of Nara and Benjamin's union had a purpose: to lift the vibration of light on Atlantis, to bring healing and harmony while sending a message to the universe to intensify the merging process of supreme love and light with Earth. We thank you all for holding the energy and space for the universe of the Creator to connect with Earth more fully, offering support and nourishment as well as sacred templates of light.

"As we foresaw, your openness to receive and share with humanity places you in the focus of the priests and priestesses of the central temples. Their focus is to create unity among all things, especially Earth and the heavens, through the process of science and machines. Such things cannot be achieved and will cause detriment to the entire energetic and magnetic structure of Earth. They are accessing all the energetic templates of Earth and the inner planes one by one, sending energies from the star beings they are guided by through the templates to mold them into one. Through manipulation, they are asking all of the energetic templates and networks as well as Earth's auric field and the inner planes to instantly transform into the Creator. Such things take time; the energetic templates and networks were not designed to merge, so all are void of their original existence. Integration and exchanges of energy occur through the templates and networks at a gradual speed because every network and template supports, grounds, or sustains something physical. It is like taking the energetic network of trees and instantly merging it with the energetic network of water; the immediate synthesis shock would kill all trees and erase water. A new creation would manifest, but it wouldn't be born from the truth of the Creator because of the lack of gradual, embedded intention aligned to the divine will of the Creator."

Benjamin and I felt our lungs slowly expanding with air and light guided by the Celestial White Beings as they grounded themselves deeper into our physical bodies. I noticed everyone in the temple was also simultaneously inhaling deeply as the Celestial White Beings encouraged us to accept their message.

"Nara, the Celestial White Beings are connecting us all as one. It is amazing! We are all like one living organism. It feels like there is no separation!" Benjamin's telepathic expression to my mind was filled with elation and exuberance. I sensed I was smiling from the very core of my being in response as the consciousness of the Celestial White Beings continued.

"In many ways, our community has the same purpose as the community within the central temples, but we choose integration of all souls and energies with the Creator to manifest the beauty of the Creator further. They are choosing integration to harness the power of the Creator to manifest their needs and desires. As a community, you are choosing to surrender to the divine flow of the Creator and let everything manifest as divinely appropriate.

"The flow of the Creator is very powerful. When you begin to manipulate the flow blockages, stagnant energy and negativity occur. Each soul on Earth is born to exist in harmony with the divine flow of the Creator, and the tendency of the ego is to access and manipulate the divine flow, which only leads you away from your divine path. The speed at which the people of the central temples wish to merge all life with the Creator templates and their intentions is creating catastrophe on Earth because the process of manifestation requires patience at a physical level. Because you brought down one of their machines when they were trying to manipulate the elemental template, the people of the central temple have been sending vibrations and frequencies of fear into the earth and directly to your community."

A strong male voice cut through the expression of the Celestial White Beings. "Is that why, after the blessing, we have felt submerged in fear — as if we are unable to escape?"

I opened my eyes quickly to see the voice was Arann's, who was sitting next to Jayda. When we were all children, Arran had studied with Jayda and me. I knew him well. Recently, he had been visiting different temples in northern Atlantis as a healer to share his gift with those in need. I took a moment to gaze at all the beautiful faces of our community members, and I felt honored that they were present with me at what seemed like an important time for Atlantis.

"Those of the central temple have been given a sound guided by star beings to bring peace to all; unfortunately, they are using the sound inappropriately, causing it to instead activate fear and negativity. They are currently emanating the sound vibration across all of humanity. You have already witnessed its detrimental effects in your community. The sound cannot be heard on a physical level, but it can be felt because it activates frustration and aggravation within to create a feeling of lack. Any person who connects with and accepts the vibration will manifest any fears they hold within. For people who are aware, this can act as a positive process of purging the entire being of fears, as they are encouraged to examine their fears without claiming to own them. Those who are not as aware of the disciplines of the spiritual path can feel overwhelmed with the fears that rise from within, identifying with them and thus energizing and manifesting them into reality, creating chaos. It is important to realize that others cannot influence you unless you allow them to. It is the same with the sound vibration that is emitting from the central temples: If you erase all fear and focus solely on love, then only love can be created. Fear, chaos, and negativity cannot be created unless they are first present or treasured within you," the Celestial White Beings responded.

"Thank you," Arann replied in gratitude and acceptance.

"We, the Celestial White Beings, give all souls present now our cleansing ray. We invite each person within this temple to sit peacefully, allow your breathing to flow naturally, and bring your attention to your heart chakra. We simultaneously place in each person's heart chakra an orb of pure white light. As you breathe into the orb, it will expand gradually and naturally, embracing your entire being and auric field. Now you exist within the orb of light and are able to receive its liquid-like cleansing vibrations moving throughout your entire being. Hold the focus of dissolving all fear and perspectives that no longer serve you. Know you will free yourself to focus and experience love in every moment of your reality while strengthening your will to exist as love. With this intention, imagine yourself swimming in the orb of light with the pure white light flowing over and through your being like the waves of the ocean. Experience your freedom, purification, and cleansing as we support you."

The entire community seemed to melt into peace and harmony as if all they were holding on to had easily been cast aside. A luscious energy manifested within the temple. It was the acceptance of freedom and trust in the divine will of the Creator — as if Earth had shook the community back into alignment. Sweetness manifested as everyone was able to receive the well of light within them once more. The Celestial White Beings began again, channeling simultaneously through Benjamin and me.

"In this state, we can now reveal the truth: There is always a divine plan created by the Creator and your souls, and this plan can alter and shift, especially as humanity is given greater responsibility over their spiritual evolution. The pathway unfolding at this moment is that Atlantis will fall sooner than we anticipated."

While channeling the Celestial White Beings, I recognized within myself and others that there was no dramatic reaction to this statement. The vibration of peace was emanating, and we were listening.

"We cannot tell you when Atlantis will fall or even if it will. The intentions and power of the star beings working with the people of the central temples is intensifying. We know that their plans and intentions, *if* implemented and manifested, will cause Atlantis to fall. Already many communities are leaving Atlantis for other countries where they plan to begin new lives in the hope of peace. Some of the communities that focused on their spiritual and inner connection with the Creator are evacuating Atlantis to preserve the wisdom and knowledge they possess for future generations. Some communities are being asked to stay on Atlantis to maintain the light and to implement healing. If Atlantis falls, these communities will be taken by us, the Celestial White Beings, and other inner plane beings into other dimensions through light travel in giant light pods designed to transport physical people, and later to such places as Egypt. We ask you as a community to stay on Atlantis to maintain the light and implement healing. Of course, there is a need for you to follow your intuition as to the appropriate pathway for your soul. We, the Celestial White Beings, will support you, whatever you decide."

Even though I was channeling, I observed the information the Celestial White Beings were imparting through Benjamin and me.

A clear, firm voice suddenly broke the silence. "Who are these star beings influencing our friends of the central temples?" Amka asked.

"The star beings cannot be named, for we do not wish this community to judge or to believe in the wrong or immoral behavior of others. We also do not wish to create a fear that could stay within your memory for generations and lifetimes to come. You know there is no need to fear star beings, for we, the Celestial White Beings, are akin to star beings. It is important for you to understand that everyone plays a role in this beautiful play that is being enacted on Earth now to deepen learning, discover the Creator, and embrace truth.

"There is no evil at work. If anything, it is the misaligned and misunderstood thoughts and perspectives of humanity. Do not paint others as wicked and yourselves as righteous, for each of you is required to discover the part your soul wishes you to play in the unfolding manifestations. Know that when you believe wholeheartedly in love — seeing, sensing, feeling, thinking, and acting as love — all will be well and manifest as the divine perfection of the Creator. There are no wrong pathways or decisions.

"Sometimes you do not understand why certain situations manifest. Often, there is no need to comprehend. Trust and attentiveness to your intuition are all that is necessary. Be attentive to love because love is eternally present within you and therefore projected around you."

Again, Amka's clear voice cut through the silence in the temple. Speaking from the heart, she asked the questions she picked up from the community. "Celestial White Beings, you have shared your warning with us. We understand we must play our part in sustaining Atlantis for future generations. I refuse to prepare for the fall of Atlantis because my preparations would only energize its creation. How can we be of service? What do you ask of us?"

"We do not ask much of you or this community, nor does the Creator. We encourage you to follow your intuition with attentiveness and hold at the forefront of your mind all the spiritual teachings you know so well. Let them be tools to sustain your inner well of Creator love. We ask that each morning you gather as a group in this temple with us to focus on a vision and hold a strong intention for harmony, love, and truth to exist on Atlantis in abundant glory once more. Chant the word 'love' together. Share your visions of the present moment and your visions of the beauty you wish to experience on Atlantis as well as between souls. Affirm together and in your alone times that love sweeps like an ocean over and through Atlantis and its people. The love of the Creator is our reality. All pain, suffering, and misalignment are erased eternally."

"We will do as you advise with great love and powerful focus," Amka communicated on behalf of us all. "We all love Atlantis; we could not bear to leave such a beautiful place. Celestial White Beings, we give you permission to divinely guide and assist us in our coming days. Let us all be tools and expressions of the Creator on Earth. We honor your presence here with us now."

Nara's Notes

We all have moments in our journey when we receive a divine warning — a message from friends, family, guides, or even a voice within — asking us to consider our path, our choices, and even our desires and needs as sacred beings of light. The warning can come in small messages or subtle experiences in your life, so it is important to listen to your intuition. It is also important to listen to the life occurring around you. Your life is your creation; any warning you experience first came from within you. To contemplate the messages of your life and the experiences shared with you is to contemplate the energies, beliefs, and intentions you create and draw from within your being.

Sometimes we can be so blinded by our desires and the need to help or succeed that we miss the warnings — and therefore miss early opportunities to change course, create a new perspective, or heal energy within. Making tweaks with these small and subtle warning messages means we do not have to experience the big warning messages when time could be running out and perspectives become harder to alter because of habit. By contemplating the messages of our reality, our lives, and the experience of our creations, we move and sway to the divine rhythm and flow of the Creator; thus, everything is easy, beautiful, and perfect. Suffering, pain, and negativity are minimized, if not erased entirely. When we become attached to our realities and experiences, unable to see the diverse pathways forward, we become stuck, resistant to the truth and unable to welcome the divine help and support always available to us from the Creator and our inner souls.

Sometimes we do not recognize the truth of certain messages because we are too attached and involved with our realities. When Amka said, "We all love Atlantis; we couldn't bear to leave such a beautiful place," she was expressing her unwillingness to let go of Atlantis, and she energized her belief in Atlantis being the only place capable of fulfilling her, thus not allowing herself to recognize other pathways available to her that could bring greater fulfillment and happiness. In some way or form, we all succumb to attachment and an unwillingness to let go and open up to beautiful new experiences. Change is a beautiful friend to embrace, but accepting change and opening yourself to contemplate all pathways available to you is also required.

There is no wrong pathway to take. You will notice this in the journey I am sharing with you. Although sometimes it may seem we are walking the wrong pathway, we can trust that it is the most perfect for us because there are no mistakes or failures — only positive learning and understanding.

Practice 24
Be Aware of Messages and Warnings

I encourage you to be aware of the messages available for you to understand in your reality, experiences, interactions, and even meditation practice. Ask yourself, "What message do I wish to make myself aware of?" Remember, the message flows from you even if it is imparted by another. You are the creator and receiver of the message.

Sometimes you also have to decipher the message. For example, maybe everyone you meet is in an angry mood. What message do you wish to make yourself aware of? It could be that there is unresolved anger within you waiting to be healed.

Notice everything occurring within and around you. Then, when you become aware of something that requires your attention, ask yourself, "What message do I wish to make myself aware of?" Allow any intuitive message or explanation to arise. Alternatively, you can start your day with that question and allow yourself to be aware of the messages your inner energy and soul place in your reality in response.

Practice 25
Listen to Your Atlantean Self

In this meditation, I encourage you to listen to your Atlantean self while realizing that to do so is to listen to yourself. Say out loud,

I now invoke the angels of Atlantis and Nara Merlyn to draw close into my auric field and surround me completely in the energy and vibration of love. I ask you to transport me to the Celestial

White Beings' temple on the northern side of Atlantis so that I may continue to reconnect or become aware of my own Atlantean energies. Thank you.

Imagine, sense, or acknowledge yourself sitting in my temple surrounded by the pure white light of the Celestial White Beings. Say out loud,

I now invoke my Atlantean self to step forth and exist before me.

Imagine or hold the focus of sending the love of your own heart into your Atlantean self as he or she exists before you. Your light flows into your Atlantean self's heart chakra and returns to you, creating a figure eight, the symbol of infinity, between you as your heart and love energy link.

With your Atlantean self existing with you, make the following request:

Please state or share three areas of your life on Atlantis that you wish to bring more awareness to. Awareness can be defined as magnification — to feel or experience more fully. For example, what three areas of your life would you like to experience more fully and therefore heal? Please share with me. I am ready to receive and listen to you.

Your Atlantean self might wish to be more connected to people, to experience love more fully, to be more in touch with her or his intuition, to heal, to be of service, to dissolve doubts, to enjoy being alive, to live without fear. There are many different areas your Atlantean self may wish to speak with you about. Know you are your Atlantean self.

You might wish to ask yourself whether the words or explanations of your Atlantean self also apply to your reality. There are always connections and patterns from other lifetimes imprinted on your current lifetime, and they are often played out without awareness. This is your opportunity to listen to, understand, and heal your Atlantean self while bringing awareness to your current reality to dissolve energetic patterns.

Take time to listen to your Atlantean self. Your Atlantean self may even speak to you by bringing forth your own memories as examples, so be open to receive your Atlantean self in any way it chooses to communicate with you. You may also wish to write down anything you become aware of.

Then create three positive affirmations connected to the three areas your Atlantean self made you aware of. If your Atlantean self speaks of dissolving the influence and power of fear, an affirmation could be,

I release fear within me and the fear projected by others. Love is my power and focus.

If your Atlantean self speaks of the desire to experience love with another, an affirmation could be,

I receive and exist in divine loving harmony with my beloved. I welcome beautiful exchanges of love in my reality.

If you already have a beloved in your life, you could instead focus on enhancing the love within your being through affirming,

Love ignites and blossoms from my soul.

Maybe your Atlantean self speaks of connection with the Creator. An affirmation for that could be,

I exist in unison with the Creator. I feel, sense, and experience the Creator within my being and reality.

Try to create three positive affirmations, saying them to yourself as often as you can each day to heal yourself and your

Atlantean self. Remember, for the affirmations to influence your reality, you need to believe in their power while truly feeling the emotions of the words you recite. What you achieve, think, experience, and feel now has an impact on your entire being. Your entire being includes all your lifetimes. An affirmation is an intention placed as a seed within your mind, energized by your soul, and projected into your reality for you to experience. An affirmation states you already have what you desire and are experiencing it in the present moment.

Allow yourself to recognize how the patterns of your Atlantean self appear in your current reality. All healing that is required and achieved with your Atlantean self instigates the same healing within your current being. You are a reflection of each other; you are one.

When you feel the process and connection has come to completion and you wish to return to your physical reality, simply invite the angels of Atlantis to ground your energies and any healing that may have taken place back into your physical reality on Earth. With each exhalation, imagine light and energy flowing from your body, through your feet, and into Mother Earth.

I am grounded, centered, balanced, and ready to continue my blissful reality on Earth.

12

The Seeding of Creation

"I am not fearful of dying," Amka said. "I just don't see the point in thinking we may die or have to leave Atlantis. Even the contemplation aids its creation." Amka raised her voice in a way I had never heard before. Always so calm and collected, she was adamant she wouldn't let Atlantis slip away without a fight.

Parlo confronted her. "The Celestial White Beings gave us a warning, Amka. Yes, they want us to help heal Atlantis and restore harmony between the spiritual and scientific sides we all possess, which are our masculine and feminine sides. However, they may have been silently preparing and asking us to let go, of our attachment to Atlantis and each other. Maybe in letting go, we will be able to exist in a more loving space to bring freedom to Earth. It feels to me that Earth is under great pressure, as if it is being molded and manipulated into something it is not by the intentions of the people of the central temples. I feel the weight of Mother Earth's pain on my shoulders.

"I also believe the people of the central temple are beginning to manipulate the template and energetic network of humans and our physical form. Many people in our community are suffering with illness. Never before has this happened. They are weakening our physical bodies."

Parlo felt as if Amka was trying to hold on to Atlantis with a too-tight grip, pushing people to meditate, visualize, and heal. "Amka, if we force situations to manifest, we are just the same as the people in the central temples. You know this. We are going against the will of the Creator and trying to control the Creator. You are aware such an energy cannot be controlled."

Parlo and Amka were standing in the center of the temple as everyone watched them with surprise. Arguments were rarely seen in our community, as we had no need to argue with each other. For four days, we had been in the temple meditating, visualizing, affirming, channeling, healing, and listening to the Celestial White Beings. Hour after hour, Amka had encouraged us to focus. We needed to rest, to observe ourselves, and to be present with our souls so we could listen and heal. Parlo was expressing our tiredness and stress while Amka was expressing a growing underlying emotion within all of us that our efforts might not be enough.

"We need to rest, Amka," Parlo said in exhaustion, letting go of his need to be right while feeling compassion for all of us.

"Let us take the remainder of the day to rest and focus on our own needs. Then we can begin afresh in the morning." I addressed the group while placing my arm around Amka's shoulders in support and understanding of her devotion and fiery will. Gratefully, everyone lifted themselves from the temple floor and made their way to the door.

Even Amka looked at me with relief. "I think I need to go to the river to cleanse my fears away. Such a long time I have spent in temples achieving initiations and mastery practices, yet I still succumb to fear," she revealed to me.

My heart instantly responded with love for Amka. It was strange to see her so fragile and unsure of herself. "You will always be our wise teacher. We do not judge you; we honor you for being so truthful with us. Forgive yourself, Amka. You are deeply loved by us. The fears we hold on to are now being challenged, as is our trust in the love of the Creator."

Parlo and Martyna waited for Amka at the temple door before departing together with the last few people. I turned to Benjamin.

"What shall we do?" I asked with excitement. It felt as if we were free and opportunities were endless.

"Well, the sun is very inviting. Would you like to join me for a walk?" Benjamin was tidying the temple as he spoke, lifting the remaining cushions into their place at the temple door.

"I would love to join you." I grasped Benjamin's hand. Closing the temple door behind us, we made our way into the woodland to enjoy the fresh air, the green nature, and the movement of our bodies as we walked side by side. We felt youthful and carefree.

We walked through the glorious, sacred trees, feeling their presence and energy embrace us as if creating a secure cocoon and pathway for us to share. The tree spirits seemed to fill us with their love as if we were a chalice. Love flowed with every breath we inhaled, burrowing deep into our beings and souls. With the supportive love of the trees, Benjamin and I deepened our connection. It was as if we were creating a bond between us while representing our energies of connection, love, and knowledge within ourselves.

The sacred chalice of our relationship was being filled with an abundant flow of supreme divine love. We were aware of the energies building within us; however, we were more engrossed in discussing and sharing our fears of the fall of Atlantis as well as our wishes to be able to restore balance between the masculine and feminine vibrations of humanity and Earth, represented through the unbalanced use of technology and spiritual evolution. We were so absorbed in deliberating the actions, intentions, and thought patterns that could create disharmony between the masculine and feminine vibrations that we did not notice the magic entwining around us as we continued walking — until we passed through the trees into a meadow.

Two beautiful butterflies danced together before us, their bodies weaving closely as if seeking oneness in every movement together. As we walked through the meadow, Benjamin and I were suddenly surrounded by numerous butterflies taking to the sky, their dance merry and united and their colors dazzling our eyes.

"They speak of union, Benjamin. They fill my mind with all variety of words to describe oneness."

"Wonderful!" Benjamin exclaimed with joy, awakening his heart further and producing the most delightful laughter.

Our energy vibration quickened. We had shared so much through our conversation that we felt content, purified, and supported entering an exquisite space of peace that every part of our beings treasured. We walked in silence, honoring the space we had created within our beings, and as a connected partnership, we experienced expansion with waves of freedom rushing through us, shifting us into altered states of perception and awareness.

As we entered a large cluster of trees, we felt as if we might explode. Benjamin expressed a need to sit down on the ground to stabilize himself. I agreed, as I felt as if I was moving into dimensions of light, escaping my body. Soon I realized my body was actually taking on more light. I gently guided Benjamin deeper into the shade and shelter of the trees to find a comfortable space to rest. Benjamin sat with his back against a tree, and I rested before him, attentive to the growing swirls of light manifesting all around us.

"Something magical is happening, Benjamin. We are so supported, guided, and loved in this moment. Nature and celestial beings are weaving a sacred geometric cocoon and grid of light around us as we rest. The trees feel like they are leaning toward us to shelter and protect us. Do you see the magical ashram forming around us — all the beautiful beings and angels of light gathering? We are so blessed! Our bodies are being infused with supreme and divine vibrations of love. My soul feels expansive; it is reaching out to you, Benjamin." Amazement emanated from my entire being.

"I see and experience it all, Nara. It is and activates within me the pure vibration of bliss. Nara, please hold my hands. Let me stay with you, for the beauty of the light surrounding us is so magnificent that my heart wants to float away."

Benjamin was trying to ground himself and to remain present with me. I encouraged him (and myself) to breathe the light we were receiving into the earth, flowing from our feet and root chakras at the base of our spines. Instantly the intensity of the light reduced as we became intensely aware of each other's presence.

"I love you, Nara," Benjamin spoke from his soul.

"I love you, Benjamin," my soul returned silently.

Before us the most beautiful golden-light chalice emerged. It was engraved with sacred light language, speaking of the truth of divine love and oneness with the Creator. The emanation of love was almost blinding. I noticed the chalice was being filled abundantly and luxuriously by a river of love. This river flowed from our souls as if creating a space for them to draw from and merge together. An intense light beam flooded all aspects of our beings from above, akin to lightning gently striking through our beings. The vibration of bliss hung in the air and radiated from every cell of our bodies. We both lifted our heads to be bathed in the celestial light of a star above us.

"I am Bliss," the star transmitted to us. "I am a celestial unification of the God and Goddess vibration of the Creator. My vibration is born from the Celestial White Beings. I am here to exist in oneness with you both and Atlantis. I hold templates and codes of the highest vibrations of harmonious love of the God and Goddess."

We could only gasp in awe. This soul was so familiar to us that it felt like an aspect of our own souls. Her beauty and sacred presence were breathtaking. The star's penetration of light through our beings began to influence our breathing patterns. As our souls engaged, our breathing became rhythmic, sending a flow of bliss up and down our spines as we became truly aware of our physical bodies and a burning fire of desire for each other that awakened from within.

We felt electric as all our senses came alive with a deep awareness of the physical and spiritual realities merging in unison. Benjamin moved his hands from my palms, caressing my arms, shoulders, and back as he drew himself closer to me. My hands began to caress Benjamin's body in a way I had never explored before: with a yearning to be closer to him, to be one with him. Removing each other's clothing, we felt the rush of light around us sink into our skin and bodies.

Benjamin gently gathered me in his arms, resting my back against the body of Mother Earth. I began to feel my breathing focus switch from my own body to Benjamin's. I exhaled love into every part of his being and inhaled the wealth of love he wished to bestow on me. I noticed our breathing synchronizing so that our energies overlapped. As our focus entered a space we both inhabited, we moved into the sacred chalice of our love. Moving in unison and with awareness, we gently merged our physical bodies as one, beginning our sacred lovemaking. Our only experience was of pure bliss. The light of the star soul Bliss infused every part of our beings with her energy.

In a moment of embrace with Benjamin with our bodies pressed together, I felt my soul and heart open further as if responding to the moment of peace. My soul brought to the forefront of my heart the most exquisite seed-like energy, so radiant and glowing with life itself. I recognized the energy instantly as the seed of creation Benjamin had told me was planted within my being from the Celestial White Beings — holding an imprint of the Creator's divine plan as well as the consciousness, wisdom, and awareness of the Celestial White Beings and their healing template. The seed of creation remained at the forefront of my heart and moved gently into Benjamin's heart chakra, where it was accepted and engulfed in his love.

Unaware of what was occurring, Benjamin gasped in delight. "I will always protect you," he whispered to me. I knew on some level he was speaking to the seed of creation newly merged with his being.

Aroused once more, we both felt the energy of the soul Bliss grounding more fully into our bodies.

"Our white beacon crystals — we must hold them," I suddenly blurted out. Benjamin reached for our discarded clothes, rummaging in our pockets until he found the white beacons. He placed mine in my left hand as a symbol of receiving and grasped his own white beacon gently.

Our lovemaking continued, quickening in speed and depth until an explosion of light filled my womb and lower chakras as I felt the celestial soul I would conceive begin her integration and physical manifestation within me. Love and bliss filled every cell of our beings, overwhelming us with joy and happiness.

The white beacons in our hands intensified with warmth, burning in our hands as they filled with the light created, the healing template of the Celestial White Beings, and the energy of harmonious and loving union between the masculine and feminine vibrations. Warmness filled my womb, and I experienced a shift within me as if the masculine and feminine aspects of my being had healed and aligned through the energy we created. We lay together, resting and drinking in the supreme energy to allow it to work with and heal our beings appropriately.

When the intensity of the energies subsided, we dressed and settled ourselves to rest, still supported and safeguarded by the trees. While sleeping, embraced in Benjamin's arms, I sensed a deep relaxation and satisfaction welling within me. So much of our stress had been relieved, and a profound healing had taken place that we could only sleep through.

Sometime later, as the sun began to set, Benjamin woke me by softly whispering in my ear. "Nara, please wake up. I want to share my dream with you. It is important, I feel."

I quickly sat up to listen to his words.

"Nara, I dreamed I was home on the star of the Celestial White Beings within a chamber of pure white light. Surrounding me were thousands of ascended masters. Some I recognized, some I did not. I felt the divine council was present, as if decisions and plans were being made. The Celestial White Beings were before me. They spoke to me very clearly, and these were their words:

"'Benjamin, we have called you to be with us, as you are the protector of the seed of creation and the Celestial White Beings' templates. There is information you are required to carry within you to support your present and future actions. Your sacred lovemaking with Nara was guided and supported by us because we needed you to truly feel oneness with each other, thus enhancing your oneness with the Creator. Many of your lower chakras were flooded with light while higher chakras awakened and activated with greater power to align you more fully to our energy and guidance. Through your acceptance of each other, your souls are ever more present, and much healing has taken place within you. You both created a supreme vibration of love that fuels your beings, filtering into Mother Earth and the White Beacons. You allowed the barriers of separation to fall away so that your God and Goddess aspects could heal, harmonize, and balance each other. The same healing and balance has filled your White Beacons, which are now programmed to project to wherever needed on Atlantis.

"'There may come a time in the future when you and Nara will feel guided to activate your merkabahs to travel into the center of Atlantis to dispense healing through the White Beacons. Please follow your intuition as the roles you play and actions you take are vital for the healing of Atlantis. With the support of the White Beacons, you will be able to share the seed of creation and our healing templates with many.

"'Benjamin, you have now received the seed of creation from Nara. It is embedded within your being; thus you both can share the energy and wisdom contained within it. We can confirm even at this early stage that Nara is now with child. The vibrations of bliss from this soul, our soul, are needed to maintain a high healing frequency and connection with the Creator within you both. This soul's energies will radiate from you both to bestow blessings of bliss to all.

"'Please value and safeguard each other, the seed of creation within you, and your White Beacons. They are important in the journey of Atlantis unfolding. We also ask you to honor the sacred healing of the God and Goddess vibrations within each of you. These can be transmitted to others.'

"The Celestial White Beings spoke for some time, but I feel I have remembered and shared the important information," Benjamin concluded.

"Surely that wasn't a dream! It was an actual experience. I can feel the power and truth of your words. I believe we began the healing process of the God and Goddess through our lovemaking. I feel whole and restored." I smiled contently.

"Nara, you are with child," Benjamin tenderly reminded me, kissing my forehead. He was unable to contain his joy.

"It is wonderful news. I am so happy! I feel we have been bestowed with many blessings. I feel completely fulfilled." I could have continued for days describing how blissful I felt, but I allowed myself to be present and aware, enjoying each sensation and moment with Benjamin.

Nara's Notes

Essentially, through our lovemaking, Benjamin and I downloaded, activated, and created a magnitude of light to serve our intention for healing within ourselves and on Atlantis. When two people have a similar intention, are aware of energy, and are in tune with their physical bodies, any form of connection — sexual interaction, a simple touch, or even breathing together — can create a powerful spiritual upliftment and activation. Sexual interactions focused on deep and pure love can open your channels to bring forth enlightenment and ascension, because it is a pure and natural expression in which the physical and spiritual merge. Even if you are simply breathing with another person with stillness and focus, energy is created between you that can fuel, support, and create your combined intention.

As humans and souls, we were designed to connect with each other — even if it's simply knowing we're connected to all things. The Creator is always within us; we are never alone. When united with others, even if just in meditation, we create energy — in truth, a magnification of the Creator. We were designed to magnify the Creator by creating, fueling, and experiencing the Creator.

It is important to dissolve the fears of connecting with other souls, people, and spiritual guides, whether on Earth or the inner planes. Fear of connection often stems from fear of being rejected. You will experience rejection only if you practice self-rejection, meaning you do not fully accept and love yourself unconditionally in your daily life. You may wish to affirm,

I allow and encourage my self and soul to connect openly, sharing my truth with divine souls of love.

When repeating this affirmation, you are also promising to dissolve judgment of yourself and others, thus cultivating loving acceptance, connection, and exchanges of any and all forms. You also might wish to ask yourself in meditation, "Do I believe that I am truly willing to share all aspects of myself with others, whether it is sexually with a partner or simply when connecting and communicating with a friend?" Do you believe you are willing to share all you are with a loved one, friend, or stranger? Would this depend on the conditions and how accepting the other person is of you? It is important to understand that your inner sense of security flows from your self-acceptance and self-love; therefore, there's no need to fear the judgment of others or self. When you practice self-love and self-acceptance in your daily reality, you can truthfully share your self with others, meaning you are willing to share — give and receive — with the Creator. Each person on Earth is an aspect of the Creator; each person is a precious jewel of life and love. With self-acceptance and self-love, you open yourself to miraculous experiences and exchanges of energy within your reality, thus magnifying the Creator more fully for your experience. Let yourself contemplate your fears of connection with others to realize how much focus you need to place on acts of self-love, such as saying, "I love myself unconditionally."

Practice 26
Download Light and Wisdom

Within the universe of the Creator and your own beings, you are able to access, download, and experience all you require to fulfill your purpose, existence, and dreams on Earth. In truth, nothing is unavailable to you, but some experiences can be more detrimental than others because they distract you from the pathways guided by your soul. When you do not yet understand the pathway your soul wishes you to proceed along on Earth, it can be challenging to determine whether an experience or intention is inappropriate or misleading. You are following your intuition more than you imagine, especially when you believe this to be true and that your actions always benefit your reality in positive, loving ways. Surrender is a wonderful way to receive; your ability to receive is essential when wishing to gain light, support, wisdom, and healing to aid your present and future actions and manifestations. I wish to share a simple exercise to support you in receiving all that is appropriate for you to accept and integrate into your reality now.

First, sit peacefully, allowing your body and mind to relax through deep breathing. When you are ready, say out loud,

Celestial White Beings, I call on your energy and pure white light to lovingly embrace me. Please support me in receiving a download of light, wisdom, healing, or inspiration to support my present and future actions and manifestations. I am open and ready to receive. Thank you.

You may have a problem or an experience that needs to be resolved and therefore wish to receive support to illuminate you further. If this is the case, after repeating the above invocation three times, hold the intention of that which needs to be resolved as being healed. Do not think of how a resolution could come forth; instead, think of the feelings of completion, understanding, and happiness.

Bring your attention to the energy of the Celestial White Beings surrounding you. Feel their white light flowing into your being with every breath you inhale. Imagine a ring of white light at your crown chakra at the top of your head. This ring transmits pure white light, wisdom, and support into your mind and entire body, downloading all appropriate light for you to receive.

If you simply wish to receive a download of light and wisdom to access inspiration without focusing on a specific area (thus allowing you to be guided by the Creator and the Celestial White Beings), simply focus for a few moments on the beauty of receiving for your highest and greatest potential after repeating the invocation above three times. Bring your attention to receiving the light of the Celestial White Beings until you can sense their presence, and do the visualization outlined above.

It is important to imagine and trust that you are receiving all you require in a form easiest for you to understand. Although you will receive instantly, it might take some time before you are able to understand what you have received. To intensify your ability to receive, you may also wish to affirm throughout your day,

I now easily receive and understand downloads of light and wisdom to lovingly support my present and future actions and manifestations.

EXTENDED PRACTICE

Invite your Atlantean self, who exists within your being and who you are eternally connected with, to download its light and wisdom to lovingly support your present and future actions and manifestations. All aspects of you have collected beautiful wisdom that is now stored within you and may need to be activated or invited forward for you to realize and comprehend. You may wish to use this invocation:

Embraced in the love and protection of the Celestial White Beings and the angels of Atlantis, I call on the energy and pure light of [Atlantean self name]. Please support me in receiving a download of light, wisdom, healing, or inspiration from you, [Atlantean self name], to support my present and future actions and manifestations. I am open and ready to receive the wisdom, light, inspiration, or healing you wish to awaken from within me, sharing with me openly. Thank you.

Imagine a ring of white light at your crown chakra at the top of your head. This ring transmits pure white light, wisdom, and support into your mind and entire body, downloading all appropriate light for you to receive.

Practice 27
The Chalice of Our Relationships

In every relationship and interaction we have with ourselves and others, energy is created that is a combined synthesis of the energy and wisdom each person is willing to share. We can imagine the combined synthesis of energy and wisdom to be a chalice, which can range from overflowing to completely dry. It is first important to notice how much you are willing to share and give to others — whether strangers or loved ones — because everything you are reflects back at you within your reality, especially your relationships.

Throughout your day, notice the different forms of relationships you create. There are relationships with loved ones, friends, animals, strangers, nature, and even your environment. If a stranger approaches you, do you hold your energy back, or do you try to be open to sharing, knowing you are always safe and protected? Do you understand this person is creating a relationship with you, a connection — if only for a moment? Do you wish for all forms of connection to be fulfilling? Do you recognize the Creator within yourself and the stranger and thus see an opportunity for magic? Do you recognize the stranger as a reflection of yourself, and wouldn't you thus like to be open to yourself?

If you are defensive and hold your energy back, the chalice between you will be completely dry. If you are open to share, to give and receive, then the chalice will fill and maybe even overflow from just a simple moment's conversation. Although you may not meet the person again, the chalice will be like a battery for you and the other person to draw from whenever you need to; thus, an awareness of having plenty and being supported will grow. This interaction fills your chalice as if you were nurturing your soul and creating a fountain of plenty to draw from within yourself.

It is about recognizing the flow and abundance of the Creator with the willingness to be of service to this flow so that you may always draw from it abundantly. Imagine the energy you can create with a loved one through a chalice that replenishes your energies and inspires you.

Simply being open to expressing yourself and accepting others allows your chalice to take care of itself. Throughout the day, try to encourage yourself to be open, communicative, accepting of others, and aware of your reactions. When you discover yourself pulling away, feeling frustrated or as if you do not have time, know this is simply resistance. Look at how you are truly feeling: Are you fearful? Or is the other person taking from you without giving in return, thus draining your chalice?

When connecting and communicating with others, consult your intuition as to what is appropriate for you in each moment. Remember that what you give is what you receive in return. Your willingness to receive also enhances your ability to give.

CHAPTER

13

Central Atlantis

We entered the temple early in the morning to find Hamna sitting in the center of the room, his legs crossed, his back straight, and his face looking very solemn. He looked up at us, and his face shifted to a light, bright smile. He rose and embraced us.

"Greetings to you, Hamna. How are you today?" Benjamin gently placed the palm of his hand on Hamna's back in a gesture of support.

"I am very well, Benjamin. I am rested and ready for another day of healing and creation. Let us hope Amka feels less insistent today." He chuckled, remembering Amka's unwillingness to let us rest.

We all laughed, but we knew Amka was only mirroring energies, emotions, and fears within our beings. We were grateful to her for courageously showing us our truths.

"Nara, you are with child! Ah, wonderful, such a joy to see," Hamna said with enthusiasm.

"How do you know?" I questioned with shock.

"I can read your aura. It has shifted in energetic pattern, and there is a new presence. I can see it plainly. The Celestial White Beings also shared the news with me this morning in meditation. I am delighted."

Something about Hamna's tone told me he wasn't delighted with the news. I had a feeling Hamna had seen the future of Atlantis — more than he would ever say — and it caused him to hold an energy of disturbance within him. A feeling of dread built within my being that seemed to rise from the pit of my stomach, gripping my body with tension and fear. Benjamin noticed my energies change

135

and moved to stand behind me with his arms wrapped gently around me. I could feel his love filling every cell of my being, allowing me to let go of the rising fear.

"We are more than delighted. We are ecstatic!" Benjamin beamed at Hamna. Nothing could dampen his spirits.

"The baby will be blessed with love from all of us. Already the baby is welcomed by all," Hamna affirmed his delight once more. "Please sit down with me. Let us all affirm the mantra shared by the Celestial White Beings. The others can join us when they arrive."

Hamna ushered us to sit facing each other in a triangle formation in the center of the temple. It seemed as if he was hiding something from us and didn't want us to question him in any way. Hamna was always an open and sharing man. He had been my teacher and guide for a long time, and I felt as if I knew him inside and out.

"Love sweeps like an ocean over and through Atlantis and its people. The love of the Creator is now our reality. All pain, suffering, and misalignment are erased eternally," we began reciting together, my tension gradually subsiding as I surrendered to the hypnotic power of the mantra.

Gradually the temple filled with friends, loved ones, and other community members who added their energy, focus, and sound to our mantra. We were united in thought and intention. I could feel waves of love flowing over my body, creating shivers up and down my spine. The Celestial White Beings danced around us, infusing our words with the love and power of the celestial levels of the Creator. The angels and archangels of Atlantis were present, and it sounded to me as if they were singing a beautiful lullaby that opened my heart and seeded vibrations of forgiveness and gratitude there.

"Let us accept and hold the vibration of forgiveness in our hearts. Let us send forgiveness to all and ourselves," I telepathically transmitted to every person in the temple. "Forgiveness is the key. Let no being be neglected. Let forgiveness be shared with all."

A great surge of peach and golden light filled the temple, swirling and caressing each of us. Building in intensity, the energy of forgiveness rushed through the temple's crystals, engaging and connecting with all of Atlantis. The energy seemed to fill me completely, as if transporting me to new dimensions of light. My third eye chakra opened wide, and I could see only Benjamin gazing at me. Benjamin reached his hand out to me, asking me to grasp it tightly.

"What is happening, Benjamin? Where have the temple and the people gone?" I telepathically spoke to him, grasping his hand so that we were together.

"We are traveling, Nara. Look around you. Our merkabahs must have activated," Benjamin shared with excitement.

Trusting Benjamin, I began to look around. Holding his hand, I felt more present and centered. It was as if we were traveling in a pod of energy. Although we had activated our individual merkabahs, they seemed to overlap, creating a cocoon for both of us to exist in. I looked behind me and could see the temple — a white beacon on the green grass — and the shimmering ocean behind it.

I recognized my surroundings. We were traveling through the air as if by magic. I didn't feel scared, as I had traveled in my merkabah with Hamna many times as a child. I recognized the feeling that my reality was both real and dream-like at the same time.

"We can go faster, if you like," Benjamin joked. He knew we could go at any speed we wished; all we had to do was hold intention.

"Are we going to the center of Atlantis, do you think?" I asked him.

"We are holding the intention and creating this experience. It must be flowing from a deep aspect of our souls, so yes, I believe we are. Can you see a great shimmering shard protruding into the sky? That is the crystal embedded within the ceiling of the main central temple of Atlantis." Benjamin pointed into the distance.

"Hamna used to say the crystal was like the earth star[1] of Atlantis. Wherever you were on Atlantis, you could feel the glow of its light."

I reminisced for a moment about the wonderful stories of the central temples. As a child, I had wished that I would one day be accepted as a priestess to work and live there.

"It doesn't seem to glow much now, does it?" Benjamin pondered. "Have you noticed that the closer we get, the darker the sky becomes? It looks as if it is almost night!" Benjamin exclaimed.

As if summoned by his words, thick black clouds surrounded us, obscuring our view. It was as if night had fallen. There were no stars, nor even the Goddess Moon. Loneliness and deprivation covered our merkabahs like a cloak.

"Get your white beacon out quickly!" I screamed as tension and shock pulsated through my body.

We both reached into our pockets, clasped our crystal white beacons, and directed the pointed ends in front of us. Centering our consciousness in our hearts, we transmitted energy into our white beacons to light our way. The

---

1   The crystal's purpose and role can be most likened to the earth star chakra in the human chakra system. Situated beneath the feet with a purpose of grounding, anchoring, and manifesting energies from the soul into the physical body, the earth star chakra supports light and consciousness in acceptance and experience. Similarly, the crystal assists in anchoring the essence of the Creator into Atlantis for all Atlanteans to access and explore.

light shone brightly, dispersing some of the dark clouds. Still, there was only the light of our beacons. We lowered ourselves slightly and began to search the land beneath us, using our beacons as torches. Expecting to see the complex labyrinth of buildings and pathways winding their way around and into the central temples of Atlantis, we instead saw rubble and debris. Piles of stones stood next to half-fallen homes and broken trees, their trunks collapsed in the middle of pathways. The clear, labyrinth-like city that had surrounded the central temples was completely derelict, abandoned by the city people.

"Something is not right here, Nara. It appears as if some kind of battle has taken place. The energy feels very compressed, fearful, and controlling," Benjamin whispered.

"I keep seeing flickering visions of people fleeing the city in fear and moving to the countryside for safety. It is heartbreaking." I tried to hold back my tears for the Atlantean people.

We flashed our white beacons forward to see the complex buildings of greater size and grandeur than the surrounding city. The shard of the central Atlantis temple crystal towered above us as we moved closer to the Great Hall and worship temples of the high priests and priestesses. We were amazed: The buildings of the priests and priestesses of central Atlantis had not been touched. They were immaculate, with gleaming outer walls.

"Power and control now reside here," Benjamin affirmed, expressing a slight feeling of dread.

We hovered in the air for some time, taking in the central temples just below us and asking our souls and the Celestial White Beings for some guidance as to what we needed to achieve or know in that moment.

"Bluebell said star beings were influencing the priests and priestesses of the central temples. They wished to create unity between the heavens and Earth through machines, perceiving it to be quicker and easier than through spiritual practices. I don't see any star beings."

I extended the beam of my White Beacon to scan the sky above the roof of the Great Hall and surrounding temples. I thought I might see a glimmer of a spaceship or some transmission flowing from the sky. I had never seen a spaceship, but I had heard many stories from people who had seen such a thing.

"There is nothing. It feels as if there is no one here anymore. It feels empty and derelict, don't you think?" Benjamin asked. "That's it!" he shouted, surprising us both. "The Celestial White Beings told us we might have to visit the center of Atlantis to dispense healing through our white beacons and maybe even share the seed of creation implanted within our beings. I feel this is why we are here, Nara."

He turned his face to me, awaiting my response. I could hardly make out his features.

"Benjamin, it's getting darker!" Shrill fear filled my voice.

"Darkness is drawing on you." I recognized the familiar tone of the Celestial White Beings. "Begin to transmit your healing light. It will guide you." They weren't around us; they needed the energy of the temple to ground their energies into the Earth plane. Instead, they were within us, guiding us through our intuition.

"Benjamin, we are the Celestial White Beings. They are within us; we *are* they — their physical manifestation. We must now show our power, our belief in ourselves as the Celestial White Beings. *We* are the White Beacons, not our crystal wands. We are the source of their healing power. We are the glowing light of purity and strength we recognize the Celestial White Beings to be. I feel they have been guiding us to this point, preparing us so that we could be united once more — united as a soul group, united as form and energy!" I exclaimed as exhilaration pumped through my being.

Benjamin squeezed my hand tightly. We both inhaled deeply and began to recite out loud, "Love sweeps like an ocean over and through Atlantis and its people. The love of the Creator is now our reality. All pain, suffering, and misalignment are erased eternally." We exhaled as if letting go of all our fears.

"We are the Celestial White Beings. We are the White Beacons of Atlantis. We are purity and love. We are limitless. And we now transmit the celestial vibrations of our soul group to heal, expose, and resolve the devastation presenting itself before us."

It felt powerful and truthful to express. Pure white light began to pulsate throughout our beings, flowing from our soul star chakras above our heads, through our hearts, and into the White Beacons we held. Visions flashed through my mind. Above me, a giant lattice network of light formed the shape of a diamond. Sacred, radiant angels surrounded the lattice. Their beauty, grace, and kindness were immense as they expressed into the lattice. I saw the Celestial White Beings cocooned within the diamond, their light shining brightly.

I gazed deeper into the diamond, amazed to see all the dimensions of the Creator's universe — all the ascended masters, rays of light, light kingdoms, stars, planets, and the entire universe of the Creator. So profound and familiar was this vision that I realized everyone was supporting us by adding their energy. The lattice of light in the diamond shape was the vehicle or channel through which the Creator's light accessed, connected, and flowed into our channels and soul star chakras. It was magical! I recognized that I was playing a key role connected to the Creator by transmitting light to dispense healing. Gratitude emanated from my heart in response to my vision, and I knew I was not important. It was because Benjamin and I had asked to be of service that this was manifesting.

The wands we held pulsed an immense and intense energy, and we gripped them tightly. Their light beams expanded far and wide and began to illuminate a metal-like pod of electricity that encased the temples. It was akin to a light bubble of protection.

"We are penetrating their protective shield with our light," Benjamin reassured me just as the entire pod collapsed and disappeared from view.

The light then moved into the temples, penetrating the walls and roofs and thus guiding our focus within. The light projected images into our minds, as if we were moving like a river of light through the buildings. Visions of large machines of different sizes, shapes, and complexities — some with embedded crystals and others with numerous wires — flashed through my mind. So unfamiliar were these objects that I couldn't comprehend their existence, let alone their purpose. They seemed to be borne of another world. Images of these machines connecting to Earth's energetic and magnetic structures flashed by. I felt Mother Earth crying in stress as her structures compressed and changed; it was as if she were caged in a new network of electricity that depleted her energies. Sadness and stress sank into my emotions.

"Get me out of here!" I screamed. "I can't do this anymore." Panic and fear filled me. I felt trapped like Mother Earth, unable to breathe or escape. "Help me!" I cried, hot tears streaming down my face. "I don't want this future," I protested. "They mean to destroy not only Atlantis but the entire world."

My mind reeled as terrifying secret files, plans, documents, and agreements were revealed to me. I couldn't understand the complexity of these files.

Voices howled at me, luring and petrifying me simultaneously. "Nara, come to us. We will show you all you need to know. Work with us. Take our power and make it your own. We mean no harm — only to merge the heavens and Earth. We have found a way of doing this that disregards the will of the Creator, and we can have what we want now! Come to us, Nara!"

I felt coldness all around me. I was falling. Benjamin was nowhere to be seen, my White Beacon obscured from my view. I hit the ground with a thud that painfully vibrated throughout my body.

"Nara, we are here to help you." The terrifying shadowy voices came again.

Then I saw them: men and women dressed in gray robes with golden chains hanging from their necks. They were all wearing the same symbol and running with determination toward me.

Fear took over my body as I tried to scramble to my feet. Darkness had surrounded me completely. I tripped and fell over rocks and rubble, feeling completely helpless.

"Help me, please!" I surrendered with all my might.

Then I heard Benjamin's voice shouting my name. Gradually the sound drew closer to me. I was in darkness and couldn't see him, but I felt his strong arms gather me to him, holding me tightly and securely. I relaxed into the safety of his presence. Benjamin's voice penetrated my mind clearly.

"That is it, Nara, relax. I am here. You are safe. You are in your temple, Nara. You are safe. Bring your consciousness back to me, to this temple, the Celestial White Beings, and your own heart, a place of sanctuary."

Light began to fill my vision, as did the reality of my temple and familiar faces gazing at me. Some looked frightened, others happy. I found myself scanning each face: Amka, Hamna, Violet, Jayda, Leesha, Parlo, Martyna, and so many more. Then there was Benjamin's concerned face looking expectantly at me. I recognized I was home.

"What happened?" I asked. "Was I dreaming?" I grasped my head, which pounded with pain and stress.

"Don't move, Nara," Benjamin said protectively. He was cradling me as if I was a baby.

I watched Benjamin as he mouthed instructions to the others. Before I knew it, I had crystals placed on and around my head to relieve my headache.

"Nara, we are placing one crystal at your third eye chakra with the intention of extracting information and visions that do not belong to you, thus clearing your mind of their presence, which is causing disharmony to the balance of your mind — as well as fear," Benjamin gently explained.

I felt people moving away from me and beginning to set up a healing intention as they transmitted pure love into my being.

"Benjamin, I need to know what happened. Please tell me; I am confused." My voice was so small and vulnerable.

Benjamin's eyes filled with love and compassion as he gazed at me. "Nara, we traveled in our merkabahs to the center of Atlantis. Our bodies remained in the temple, yet we were real — almost in physical form — as we traveled. We began to transmit healing into the temples to dissolve and reveal all present energies.

We penetrated their bubble of protection with our light, which alerted them to our presence.

"Suddenly you started to move about violently within our united merkabahs. You were shouting so much, as if you were processing or accessing their secrets and plans for the future. I tried to calm and soothe you, but there was nothing I could do. You seemed to lose the strength of light within your merkabah, and you fell to the ground. I could see men and women dressed in gray coming toward you. It was all too much to witness, so I just held the intention of us both being fully back in the safety of the temple, and I found myself here holding you in my arms. You have been unconscious for a little while. It is as if you mentally absorbed everything they were hiding and all their goals. Whether they wanted you to see them or not, I don't know. It was certainly frightening."

"So it was real?" I asked again, unsatisfied.

"Yes, Nara," Hamna interrupted, his face appearing before me. "You visited the central temples energetically and experienced everything in your lightbody. Your visions are the truth. I am sorry for your experience." Tears flooded into his eyes. "We are clearing your mind now and healing the fear from your body," he gently reminded me.

"What was the purpose of this experience?" I asked Hamna and Benjamin.

"The purpose was to anchor healing while revealing the truth of what has been occurring in the central temples. You also dissolved their defenses and absorbed all their plans, goals, and intentions, which means we can now heal them. We are not only dissolving them from your mind but also downloading them into a crystal so that they can be erased and terminated completely from the crystal, their reality, and the reality of Atlantis. Without their plans and goals, their power and impact on Earth and Atlantis will be depleted.

"Nara, I knew this morning that this was the plan of the Celestial White Beings. They knew that as a channel you would be able to easily absorb the necessary information, so they sent you to central Atlantis with your protector, Benjamin, to mentally absorb the plans and mental creations of the priests and priestesses, diminishing their power.

"When we wish to manifest anything, we create a vision. This vision is energized and begins to create a pathway of increasing energy into the physical realms to complete manifestation. Because you absorbed their visions, we have now dissolved the energetic pathways already set up for their manifestations, and they will have to begin again. Do you understand?"

Hamna's face drew closer to me as I continued to lie in Benjamin's arms.

Before I could respond, Hamna placed his index finger on my third eye, causing everything to dissolve before me as I fell into a deep, peaceful sleep.

Nara's Notes

Sometimes the beings of light supporting us share only part of the picture or greater plan for our realities. This is because we have multiple opportunities available to us in every given moment. If they were to share everything that could occur in our realities, all the possibilities in the present and future, they would affect our experience of life and our understanding of spiritual lessons, taking away our free will to choose. They do not conceal information from us; instead, they protect us from the pressure of knowing the whole plan of the Creator and want us to follow our intuition to find a clear pathway forward that suits our needs. It's much easier to deal with the unknown when you take it step by step.

We always have free will on Earth, although it often doesn't seem that way. It can appear as if situations happen to us without our control. Whatever occurs in your reality, whether small or large, positive or negative, it is wise to remember that somewhere in your life, even if it is in the distant past, you consented to the experience. Your consent can be a fearful thought in the past or a wish to be of service. Your thoughts, beliefs, and perspectives of the past and present are projected into your reality. Your guides then intertwine the divine will of the Creator, who always tries to generate harmony and love in your reality as inspiration supporting you in fulfilling your sacred purpose. Acceptance is the key to life, and when you accept that at some point you consented to your current experiences (often unconsciously), then you are more easily able to move through and learn from them.

Just as you can't hold a red-hot rod, you can never hold on to blame. You cannot give blame away to others either, as it will hurt them (or you) further as you observe their turmoil. You have to let go of blame and no longer tolerate its presence. I could have blamed the Celestial White Beings for not telling me the whole truth and for placing me in a dangerous situation, but I did not. I knew I had asked to be of service in any way I could, I knew I was always safe and protected, and more than anything, I knew everything was always appropriate and well in my life.

Even though I panicked and felt fear rush through my body, there was knowingness of my safety.

Even when this knowingness comes afterward, it is very powerful, important, and influential. This is to say that whatever happens, I learn to accept it and cultivate love within my being, which dissolves all blockages and acts as a magnet to positive, loving experiences.

When you blame another, your guides, or even the Creator, you are stating that you know best, that you have all the answers and your perceptions are the most accurate. This only causes you more pain, as you will never allow yourself to see the perfection of the Creator. The perfection of the Creator is within all situations, experiences, and people. When we have belief and understanding, we know the story we are weaving with the Creator has not yet finished for us.

It is important to know that (and hold faith in) the wisdom and guidance of your guides and intuition always are appropriate in the moment of asking. Check back with your guides or your intuition regularly because as you evolve and change, the guidance alters and shifts. It is important to be aligned with your present intuition and guidance rather than hold on to guidance of the past, which may no longer apply. Remember, you only receive the wisdom and guidance appropriate for you to understand and act on. Focusing on the desire for more understanding and knowledge of how things will actually pan out or what exactly you need to know will only distract and block you from receiving greater wisdom. Again, it comes back to trust and acceptance.

You accept your power when you know all truth is revealed to you in divine timing. If you also affirm that you are always ready to receive the truth of the Creator — whether it flows from guides, loved ones, or situations in your reality — you know you will always be supported in dealing appropriately with the truth. No one wants to live in a world of illusion, so we constantly seek the truth of the Creator. To accept it, sometimes we have to let beliefs go or know in advance that we are strong, courageous, and able to overcome any and all situations in a manner of love, peace, and harmony. This way, we are content with all aspects of our reality at all times. You may wish to affirm in your daily life,

I am strong, courageous, and able to move through all and any situations in a manner of love, peace, and harmony. I now accept the truth of the Creator.

There was a very beautiful moment when I simply accepted myself as a Celestial White Being. This realization gave me power as if I was seeing myself as my truth for the first time. Delving deeply, I drew my truth to the surface to support and be of service. You can do this in your everyday life; you don't even need to know who your soul group is or what the origins of your energy are. You do, of course, know you are the Creator and all that is the Creator. Just affirming, *"Today, I accept myself as the Creator"* is a very powerful process. Everything you wish to be is already within you. Whether you wish to be abundant, fearless, courageous, strong, compassionate, or healthy, there is a need to accept that it is already within you. Accepting is drawing the reality of your truth into manifestation. So let the affirmation *"I accept my _____"* be a part of your everyday dialogue with yourself. Overcome your fear by accepting your truth: You are all that is the Creator.

Practice 28
Clear Outdated Mental Patterns and Manifestations

We are all subject to influence from the outside world, thoughts of others, and even vibrations of fear that may be focused on humanity to instill control. Meditating and choosing what we wish to think can overcome this. We also are affected by our past-lifetime selves — the thoughts, plans, and goals they created. These can reoccur in our current lifetimes when they are really not needed simply from a lack of clearing and cleansing the mind of outdated mental patterns and onset manifestations.

At any given time, we think many different things, and when thoughts become similar, they create an energy that snowballs in our lives. The speed of manifestation depends on the number of like thoughts and our emotional investment. Many thoughts we put into the process of manifestation are not needed because they act as distractions in our lives. Rather than combing through your thoughts one by one — which would be of great assistance and insight to you, although difficult — when you wish to clear past-lifetime mental patterns, practice the following invocation as many times as you wish:

Beloved Celestial White Beings, my guides, my soul, and the Creator, I call you forth to cocreate a deep healing and cleansing process concerning my mental patterns and manifestations. Let your light of supreme love and purity pour into my entire being, especially my mind, brain, thoughts, mental body, and all aspects of myself, aiding and creating my thought and manifestation process on Earth.

Please appropriately heal and erase all thought patterns and creations put into the process of manifestation (at whatever stage they may be) to be created by my Atlantean self that are no longer required or that no longer serve or support me in my life and ascension. Even if these thought patterns, creations, goals, plans, or mental attachments have weaved their way through many of my lifetimes, if they are no longer needed or appropriate, let them be healed and dissolved with harmony and well-being restored in all areas. A deep purification is now occurring with my consent, as guided and overseen by my soul, resulting in a positive, fulfilling, and empowering outcome. Let me, my Atlantean self, and all aspects of my soul be free from the unneeded thoughts and creations of my Atlantean self.

Please appropriately heal and erase all thought patterns and creations put into the process of manifestation (at whatever stage they may be) created by me in my current reality that are no longer required or that no longer serve or support me. Even if these thought patterns, creations, goals, plans, or mental attachments have weaved their way into my future or into the cellular level of my being, if they are no longer needed or appropriate, let them be healed and dissolved with harmony and well-being restored in all areas. A deep purification is now occurring with my consent as guided and overseen by my soul, resulting in a positive, fulfilling, and empowering outcome.

I am free from outdated mental patterns and manifestations. I accept this process of healing and expansion within my being. Thank you.

Sit peacefully for at least ten minutes, as this will allow the energies to work with you. With every breath you exhale, say in your mind, "I let go."

Practice 29
Cultivate Balance between the Outer and Inner Power

On Atlantis, we are very aware of the balance between outer power and our inner power. Outer power doesn't belong to us; it might have been created by us through our creativity or intellect, but it serves as a tool that we are not attached to in any way, and it can support our realities at a physical level. This is defined as a tool, machine, or device that supports us in achieving something or empowers us in our daily lives.

Your inner power belongs to you. It is unique to you, and although it is brought forth from the Creator, it is expressed through you. In truth, you cannot detach from your inner power. You can ignore it, but that leads to sadness. Your inner power is limitless; with it, you can attract all you need and desire into your reality to serve you. It is your essence that is expressed through your mind and emotions to manifest and attract all you require.

When you are aware in times of challenges or need, you first look to your inner power for support, courage, belief, healing, or intuition. These are all your inner power manifesting in many wondrous ways. When you attach to outer power in times of challenge, you look for inspiration, support, or guidance from the outer world, bypassing your inner power or deeming it insufficient. This disempowers you instantly, resulting in missed opportunities with a growing reliance on others and technology.

In your current reality, you might recognize that both are

needed; however, a balanced is required. Take time to contemplate your reality. Do you rely heavily on technology and resist the power within you? Do you ask yourself for inspiration, healing, and guidance while resisting the help offered to you from outside? Do you need to make more time in your life to sit silently and relax without any other outer distractions? If all of your technology were taken away, how would you feel? If you were to live without any form of technology, how would you feel if people gave you gifts of technology to enhance your life?

You might also wish to contemplate whether in times of challenge you are in a habit of tuning into your own power for guidance or into the power outside of you, such as other people or devices.

The key is to acknowledge where resistance lies, as it is the alert of balance not being present. If you resist technology, why? If you resist meditation, taking time for yourself, or even just relaxation, why? What are you fearful of, and how can you achieve balance in your everyday life?

Take time to contemplate your inner and outer power balance. You may also wish to consider what message the technology you use is giving you: Is it a message of power or disempowerment? You may wish to create a routine time in each day to just sit without any form of distracting technology.

This may seem like an unusual request to bring about balance between your spirituality and the technology in your life; however, you will see in my story the impact and power unbalanced attachments can have on a whole civilization. There are powerful similarities between the experience of Atlanteans and your reality now. I believe spirituality and technology have yet to find balance in your current world.

14

The Preparation

Drifting into consciousness, I came back to my physical body and opened my eyes to the sound of chanting swirling through my ears and my mind, and even being spoken hypnotically from my mouth. I gradually recognized the words as the mantra presented to us by the Celestial White Beings: "Love sweeps like an ocean over and through Atlantis and its people. The love of the Creator is now our reality. All pain, suffering, and misalignment are erased eternally." The chanting continued, the sound growing as the power of all present expanded.

Benjamin's face appeared before me.

"Nara, you are awake? I have been affirming and visualizing this moment. Thank you, Creator." Benjamin wrapped me in his arms and squeezed me tightly.

His gratitude shocked me. "What has happened, Benjamin? Why am I lying in the center of the temple floor?"

"Oh, Nara, you have been unconscious for five days since our experience of traveling to the center of Atlantis. I have been questioning the Celestial White Beings profusely, wanting to understand what was happening. They simply told me to trust and that you would awake with divine timing. I felt it best to leave you in the temple so that the Celestial White Beings could heal you. I have been by your side day and night."

Benjamin's eyes were welling up with tears. I could feel him letting go of his anxiety now that I was present once more.

"Benjamin, I am really sorry I haven't been present with you. I feel well now. Let me stand up." I recognized twangs of guilt appearing within my being for leaving Benjamin and my community at a time when they needed me most. I felt as if I had let them down, although I knew I must have been needed on the inner planes to help Atlantis.

My sadness was consoled by the beautiful and grateful faces greeting me — the physical faces of my community and family. I was embraced lovingly as they helped ground me back in my reality. As my heart expanded, I felt radiance and vitality fill my being. I gradually made my way to the door of the temple, seeking some fresh air. As I opened the door, I was shocked to see only blackness ahead of me. Benjamin was close behind me.

"Is it nighttime?" I asked, somewhat disappointed.

Benjamin looked at me. There was silence between us as he waited, hesitation and awkwardness emanating from his body. Stepping outside, I was greeted with a pungent odor rather than the familiar scent of fresh sea air. No stars were visible in the sky. The darkness seemed impenetrable, and it clung to my body like toxic smoke. I stepped backward, pushing Benjamin back into the temple, and I shut the door firmly. Looking around, I noticed bedding, food, and belongings all piled up next to the white wall of the temple.

"Everyone is living in the temple!" I whispered intensely to Benjamin. "What has happened? Please tell me the truth."

Benjamin drew me close to the closed door as if to conceal and separate us from the others. "The Celestial White Beings invited us to gather all we would need to remain in the temple for a few days. This was before thick clouds began to flow from central Atlantis in our direction. The clouds began as white but quickly turned gray and then black, surrounding the temple completely. It is like a thick black fog out there now. Some of the group have tried to move through it, but they became disoriented and confused, and the toxic smell overpowered their senses. We are grateful to be together in the temple as guided by the Celestial White Beings; however, we have no idea what is occurring. I can only guess Atlantis is falling and the Celestial White Beings are preparing to transport us to Egypt as promised." Benjamin looked hopeful, yet I could see his normally strong inner presence, power, and belief had been knocked by recent circumstances.

Benjamin's words shocked me but made perfect sense, as they felt very familiar and appropriate at the same time. I felt a knowingness of all being well within me and simply wanted to transfer this to Benjamin. Maybe this was why I had been unconscious for so many days — I did not know. I did, however, know my entire body wished to embrace Benjamin and hold him closely and lovingly. I felt much of Benjamin's stress and tension flow away as I activated the energy of the seed of creation and the Celestial White Beings within me, radiating it to

Benjamin to bring his entire being back into complete and absolute alignment and balance with his truth.

I felt Benjamin's energy respond to me instantly, building and returning to his expanded, powerful self. Our light merged, and golden white light began to shine in all directions, filling the temple with vibrations of harmony, peace, truth, and love — the love of two soul mates, a love that honored the Creator within. Everyone's attention in the temple switched to us as they bathed in the grace and love of the Creator we were channeling and radiating, which began with a simple, loving embrace. People began to weep — some quietly and gently, others sobbing intensely as the fear, insecurity, uncertainty, and tension that had been building within them crumbled away. The atmosphere in the room lifted and shifted to vibrations of love and grace. Releasing Benjamin from my embrace, I turned to see the luminous white energy of the Celestial White Beings enter the temple, gently holding all in their pure love.

Benjamin slid his back down the wall of the temple to sit on the floor and guided me to sit before him, my back leaning against his strong chest. People who were gently weeping, allowing a deep release to take place, gathered closer. Jayda sat before us with his arms protectively enfolding Leesha. Their presence symbolized to me that the masculine and feminine vibrations were balancing within the temple, which was needed to encourage us to soar into a state of oneness with the Creator. Parlo sat with his arms around Martyna and Amka, holding them closely. Violet leaned into Hamna as he embraced her in his loving arms. Every woman in the temple was embraced by a man, and my eyes took in this tender and symbolic moment.

Not only were we creating balance between the masculine and feminine vibrations, but the feminine vibration was being protected, cradled, cherished, and in some cases, hidden for safety. Was this a symbol for the future, a preparation for the coming circumstances? Would the divine power of the feminine need to be protected in times to come by the power of the masculine? The masculine vibrations within all demonstrated an intense power that might disempower the divine feminine, but in truth, it was to tenderly safeguard the divine feminine and her sacred treasures until they could be revealed and restored once more. Such thoughts and questions ran through my mind, and all I could do was simply let them go. All I knew for sure was that a deep love filled the temple, showering blessings on us all.

The energy and vibration of the Celestial White Beings subtly entered my mind and moved through my body as they prepared to channel through me to address us all.

"Magnificent beings of light, we honor you now and send our love to embrace you warmly. Please know we are with you in your hearts and souls, eternally protecting and guiding you. We come forth to you with love because we have some news to share with you.

"Atlantis is falling. We have stated this to you before, but now this statement is truly evident on Earth. Your dedication to the light and healing expressed to all has sustained Atlantis for a period and counteracted some of the misguided work of others. You have also safeguarded some of the Atlantean consciousness and memories of Atlantis, which will be held within your souls and reseeded into the consciousness of humanity in civilizations to come."

Those around me released a sigh of despair. I felt their relief that the Celestial White Beings were present once more to guide and explain all that was occurring to us.

"As the machines created by the priests and priestesses in the central temple of Atlantis interfere with the magnetic field, they are causing destruction to the flow of the magnetic field from north to south, drawing the magnetic field's flow into Atlantis and creating a massive vortex. The vortex is like a whirlwind that expands hundreds of miles, but unlike a whirlwind, it is sucking in dust, debris, and pollution from the atmosphere into its walls, then carrying it as a strong high wind along and around the surface of the entire Earth. Due to the current expansion of the vortex, you exist within its eye, so all is calm. You are experiencing the black, toxic smoke, which is a buildup of all the vortex is sucking inward. The entire Earth is experiencing the same thing with the addition of freak and volatile winds that are causing havoc.

"Many people blame the weather, as they are unaware of what is occurring on Atlantis. As the winds build, they create a cycle of flow from Atlantis along the surface of Earth and return to Atlantis to be sucked in once more. The vortex will become smaller as the magnetic fields are manipulated further. As the vortex narrows the power of the magnetic field, you will be able to punch a hole in the ground through Atlantis and into the center of the Earth. On the other side of the planet, the magnetic field will be unable to complete its cycle, being drawn inward to meet the force flowing through Atlantis into the earth. Thus the magnetic poles of Earth will shift."

My mind was spinning with the words and images the Celestial White Beings were channeling through me. I could hardly comprehend what they were conveying to us, but I invited them to continue, hoping they would bring further understanding and clarity.

"The manipulation of the magnetic fields will create catastrophic effects for Earth's tectonic plates, causing them to shift and slip, triggering tsunamis. The planet will alter beyond recognition. If the magnetic field is no longer activated, all of humanity will lose their memories. You can see the devastation unfolding now for Atlantis, Atlanteans, all of humanity, Earth, and the universe of the Creator. At worst, we will experience the destruction of all of creation. At best, we will be able to manage the energies of Earth that would result in a magnetic pole change in which Atlantis would become the South Pole of Earth after all energies are sucked into it. For this to occur, the magnetic field of Earth would need to be restored to bring structure and stability to the planet once more. The magnetic field is necessary for souls to walk on the planet in physical bodies."

Hot tears began to roll down my cheeks. I couldn't hold my compassion and sadness for humanity and Mother Earth inside any longer.

"Nara, it is important for you to continue." Benjamin squeezed my hands tightly as he sat behind me, our torsos pressing against each other for comfort and emotional support.

I inhaled deeply and let go of my sadness, allowing the Celestial White Beings to continue their communication through me.

"We have shared before the purpose of the priests and priestesses. They wish to dissolve separation, merge heaven and Earth, and merge all energetic bodies into the physical, thus manifesting the Creator fully and instantaneously on Earth. It has yet to dawn on them that through their instant manifestation of the Creator they are actually destroying Earth and the entire universe of the Creator, as if reversing time, manifesting once more the original manifestation of the Creator. Thus all of creation will be erased. Without awareness, they are creating a black hole.

"Please know that all on the inner planes are lending their energy and consciousness to bring forth the Creator's divine plan to dissolve all destruction. We will return to you and create a merkabah for your community to enter. We will safeguard you on the inner planes, containing you within our energy. This means you will retain your memories and your physical bodies. When the time is appropriate, we will return you to Earth, to the country of Egypt, to continue your life cycles.

"Now is the time to be in love free from fear, blame, or anger. Love will sustain you eternally. We surround you within a ring of angelic beings. Know this temple is a sacred and protected space for you. Please await our return."

The energy and consciousness of the Celestial White Beings left my body, and as I opened my eyes, I saw their mist-like white energy disappear from the temple.

"They have gone," I said to the group.

"All those visions I had about Mother Earth — her pain and suffering as well as the disappearance of Atlantis — it has all come true," Hamna said, devastated, his head resting in his hands. "Atlantis will be forgotten, erased from the history of humanity," he mumbled.

"Hamna! Everyone!" Jayda interrupted, "our greatest tool in this moment is acceptance. We have to accept that we played a part in the fall of Atlantis, accept on some level that it is our choice to experience everything unfolding for us now. With acceptance, we can rekindle our strength and see with clarity the truth of this matter and the larger picture that our souls hold for us to receive and embrace. We are going to be together throughout this entire process. Yes, the land of Atlantis may no longer caress our feet, but we have the greatest gift of all: We are together. Our lives will continue, and we can share and experience together, supporting each other."

Jayda's broad smile tried to reach everyone in the room, lifting them back into truth. Amka joined him.

"Jayda is right. We are required to let go of our attachment to Atlantis, our beloved home. We will create a new home together in Egypt, and the spirit of Atlantis will live on within our beings." Amka paused in thought. "Let us celebrate! Let us sing songs, share stories, and dance, feeling our bodies enthused with the life force energy of the Creator."

Amka gazed at each person in the group, but she realized they did not yet fully accepting her words or plan of action. "Jayda, get out your musical instruments, your crystal singing bowls."

Jayda jumped to his feet at Amka's command.

Resting my back on Benjamin's chest, I felt him clear his throat. His beautiful voice began to resonate throughout the temple, singing, "Although the wind, the wind will blow, let your light shine bright. Although the rain, the rain will fall, let your love shine bright. Although the storms, the storms will come, let your peace guide you home, for the sun, the sun will shine, and embrace you forever more."

Nara's Notes

For us, this was such a soul-searching time. Everything was changing, and we were asked to place our complete trust in the Creator and the Celestial White Beings. We were asked to put into action all the beliefs we created, the spiritual practices we achieved, our learning, and the spiritual growth of our entire lifetime so that they could become our truth. In many ways, every soul on Earth experiences a moment like this when everything you know — all your foundations, everything you have dreamed of — falls away, leaving you to feel as if you have nothing or the journey of life has no purpose. Whether on a small or large scale, there is a purpose for clarifying your beliefs and focusing on what matters to you.

Life on Earth is not eternal. Throughout the journey of life, we are asked to let go, to dissolve our attachments to life and embrace its truths and our own beings. Love is eternal and can never truly be broken or damaged. Your soul transforms, expands, and evolves, which is its greatest joy, so change is inevitable. There is always a divine plan, always a positive outcome, always inspired understanding that dawn if you allow yourself to move with the divine flow of the Creator. We chose to hold on to love and our faith in the Celestial White Beings and the Creator. Love and faith are all you can truly hold within your being and express to others.

Practice 30
Your Personal Experience of the Fall of Atlantis

For many souls on Earth who are continuing what was not completed in Atlantis in their current lifetime, the fall of Atlantis can be a healing that needs to take place because it is often a wound within your heart that can project into your current reality. A wound of pain, suffering, or fear from the fall of Atlantis can manifest in numerous ways that can be recognized through your belief systems. Maybe you feel that nothing ever works out and that you are unable to trust others or yourself. Maybe you dislike technology or feel the prospects of evolution and ascension on Earth are hopeless. You might feel resentment; blame; lack; or fears of the world coming to an end, of death, or of drowning. An experience such as the fall of Atlantis can bring up many energies and feelings, especially profound loneliness. Now is the time to give yourself and your Atlantean self the opportunity to let go of any pain, suffering, or wound so that you can bring forth deeper healing. You might even be reading my words because that is your need this very moment — to release and heal old pain and wounds. Say out loud,

I now invoke the angels of Atlantis and Nara Merlyn to draw close into my auric field and surround me completely in the energy and vibration of love. I ask you to transport me to the Celestial White Beings' temple on the northern side of Atlantis so that I may continue to reconnect or become aware of my own Atlantean energies. Thank you.

Imagine, sense, or acknowledge yourself sitting in my temple surrounded by the pure white light of the Celestial White Beings. Say out loud,

I now invoke my Atlantean self to step forth from within me to share any needed information or insights. Atlantean self, please share with me your experience of the fall of Atlantis, if it is divinely appropriate. I am ready to hear, sense, or acknowledge your thoughts, visions, memories, insights, feelings, or anything else you wish to share with me. The purpose of my connection with you is to bring forth a deep healing. I am ready to receive and listen to you.

Take time to listen to your Atlantean self. Your Atlantean self may even speak to you by bringing forth your own memories as examples, so be open to receive in any way he or she chooses to communicate with you. You may also wish to write down anything you become aware of. When you have a feeling, sensation, or knowingness of the presence of your Atlantean self, you may wish to ask these questions:

- *Was my Atlantean self present in the temple with Nara during the fall of Atlantis?*
- *What did my Atlantean self experience at the end of Atlantis?*
- *What healing, if any, needs to be addressed, released, and transformed in connection with the fall of Atlantis?*

You can either ask these questions out loud singularly and with patience or write them down, remaining aware of any insights or feelings flowing into you, and document them if you wish. Give yourself plenty of time, space, and quietness to simply be, allowing any energy that needs to unfold to do so in its own time.

Know that remembrance can come in pieces, and you might have to patch them together. Know that if you do not receive any insight, it may not be the most appropriate time, or you may have a fear or some resistance to understanding the truth. Breathing in and out gently while you focus on love will always heal any energy or experience. It is important to accept any insights free from judgment of yourself or your Atlantean self, meaning you should try not to take it personally. It is simply an aspect of healing that is required to take place and in no way diminishes your divinity or worthiness of existing as an expression of the Creator.

Practice 31
A Clear Perspective

It is important to understand that everything in your life is a process. Know that uncomfortable situations will pass and no experience is eternal. This knowledge and understanding brings comfort while allowing you to let go of all that is no longer needed. You can move through any uncomfortable situation or experience with greater ease by asking yourself the question,

What do I now need to release to return to love?

You can write this question down, documenting whatever

comes to your mind. When we know that each situation is a process, we understand the energy will pass and new experiences will enter our lives; thus, we are connected on a deeper level with the flow of the Creator, stopping us from becoming stuck in a certain energy, understanding, or experience.

I encourage you to choose an affirmation from the list below. I invite you to repeat the affirmation, calling on your Atlantean self to be with you so that you can infuse the energies created by the repetition of the affirmation into your current reality and Atlantean self, which will promote healing. Try repeating the affirmation out loud for ten minutes.

- *Everything in my physical reality is the perfection of the Creator.*
- *I embrace an understanding of the greatness of the Creator manifesting in my life each day.*
- *I allow everything in my life and all my creations to be aligned with love.*
- *I move through my physical reality with ease and perfection.*
- *I always experience beautiful and loving experiences.*
- *Every moment is a beautiful transformation for me.*

15

The Fall of Atlantis

"When do you believe the Celestial White Beings will come to collect us?" Leesha anxiously asked Martyna.

"Very soon, I am sure, Leesha. We must trust in their promise to us." Martyna gently placed her arm around Leesha's shoulders to comfort her.

I had overheard such conversations many times since the channeling from the Celestial White Beings. Everyone wanted to know when the Celestial White Beings would return. Anxiety and impatience were building in the temple as people continually opened the door to check the outside conditions, which were becoming extremely wild. We sang our songs, shared our stories, danced, and slept for what felt like an eternity. We were ready to leave Atlantis now, but the Celestial White Beings were not ready to collect us. Benjamin and I spent time praying to the Celestial White Beings for their return as soon as possible, creating intentions, and visualizing our community being transported to safety.

Benjamin turned to me and gazed straight into my soul. "Nara, I feel this is a test, a challenge to hold and maintain our faith. I feel we must let go of our expectations of how and what the will of the Creator should look like and exist in our reality. It is time to dissolve our expectations, knowing all is well and surrendering to the divine will of the Creator."

"I believe you are correct, Benjamin. We trust in the Celestial White Beings, so there is no reason to lose our faith." I looked around the temple and could see that many people were losing their faith. "I feel helpless and responsible, Benjamin. How can we console them?" An air of desperation filled my voice.

"Let us join everyone together. We need to maintain a strong unity within our group." Benjamin reached for my hand and squeezed it tightly as he raised his voice. "Everyone, let us gather together to enhance our unity. Let us focus on love, peace, and joy as we invite the Celestial White Beings to return to the temple."

People took their places in a circle. Benjamin smiled at me, pleased his plan was working out. The only person who didn't join our circle was Ela, a teenage girl with long blond hair and a very pale complexion. She was tall and seemed ethereal and angelic. She spoke softly, and her pale-green eyes reminded me of an Atlantean meadow. Originally from the southern side of Atlantis, Ela had been studying with Amka for a few years and was to remain under Amka's care until she perfected the ways of the priestess. Ela's back was toward us.

"Ela, will you join us?" I asked quietly, seeing tension taking hold of her shoulders. There was no answer. "Ela, we would be honored if you would join us," I said, moving closer to where she stood and placing my hand gently on her back.

"I will not!" Ela roared at me. She turned to me, her face radiating red-hot anger and fear. Her anxiety rippled out of control as it moved through her body.

"Everything is in divine order, Ela. You are safe and loved by us." I paused, but she didn't respond. "I know you must be concerned about the well-being of your family and friends, not being with them at this time," I whispered gently.

Ela roared at me once more. "I do not trust you. I do not trust the Celestial White Beings. They will not come for us. They have tricked us, and they are leaving us to die. I do not want to be with you all any longer!" Ela ran to the temple door, throwing it open with all her might and racing into the storm outside. Winds hauled through the temple door, the noise eerie and threatening as it cast debris and water onto the temple floor. I ran to the temple door.

"Ela, come back! It isn't safe for you to be out there!" I shouted into the chaos unfolding around the temple.

"What do we do?" Amka pleaded. "Ela is under my care."

"I will search for her, Amka. She can't have gone far, I am sure," Martyna assured Amka.

"Martyna, no!" I shouted as she ran out of the temple door followed by two other ladies from the group.

Parlo and three other men then ran out of the temple door shouting to the others to return to the temple. Women and children started to scream as the foundation of the energy and security created by the group diminished. Amka slumped onto the floor in despair and disbelief at what was unfolding around her. People gathered around Benjamin and me, screaming for us to help them as their anxiety rose and hysteria manifested.

"Nara, I must go and find the others!" Jayda shouted to me passionately over the panic-stricken noise forming in the temple.

"Jayda, I will not let you go out there. Martyna and Parlo have already gone. I can't lose you as well. Please stay, Jayda," I begged, grasping for his arm and missing as he approached the temple door. He looked back at me, his eyes fixed on mine and filled with a mixture of adrenaline and regret before he vanished into the darkness.

I could see my own fears of loneliness and loss manifesting before me. I recognized how ugly and false they were, yet they captivated my mind.

The temple door began to swing wildly and crash against the wall and the door frame as the conditions outside worsened.

"This is hopeless, Benjamin. What do we do? This is too much." I ran to Benjamin, pounding his chest with my fists as I filled with anger and rage. Hysteria was awakening within me in a reflection of everyone's reactions around me.

Benjamin pulled me close to him, wrapping his arms around me in a restraining embrace. "Be at peace, Nara. No problem is ever resolved through anger and rage."

With Benjamin's words, I found my center and returned to my peaceful, loving heart as I let go of my fears and focused on my breathing, all tension pouring from my being. I began to cry, my sobs muffled by Benjamin's chest. A part of me felt alarmed by my reactions.

"Stay with me, Nara. Everything is going to work out well. Trust me," Benjamin reassured me.

Then we heard it, a noise we had been passionately waiting for: the sound of the crystal in the ceiling vibrating as the Celestial White Beings entered the temple. Silence and stillness spread across and through every person in the temple as we all looked up in amazement to watch the white mist swirl into the temple with ease and perfection. The white light began to form a large and expansive bubble in the center of the temple that encapsulated us all. It was the Celestial White Beings' merkabah.

"They have come to collect us!" Benjamin shouted with exhilaration.

Everyone huddled closer together to ensure they existed within the white merkabah. Safety, it seemed, had come, and no one wanted to be left behind.

"You must activate your own merkabah as well, linking it to the merkabah created by the Celestial White Beings," Benjamin advised as he drew me closer to what remained of our gathered community, trying to ensure my safety and protection.

162 • White Beacons of Atlantis

I felt myself pull away from Benjamin firmly. "What about the others, Benjamin? We must help them!" I was shocked by his disregard for the others who had left the temple.

"Please stay in the merkabah, Nara!" Benjamin shouted. "Think of our baby! The Celestial White Beings will return for the others."

Benjamin's firm gaze only caused me to move farther away from him. I did not recognize the man in front of me, nor did I know what I was doing. I knew I couldn't leave the others behind; I felt responsible for everything occurring, and such deep feelings of regret, distrust, and guilt were rising within me. I stepped out of the merkabah, gazing at Benjamin and the others. Benjamin came toward me, but I ran toward the temple door. Hesitating, I looked back at him and ran straight into Jayda, who came tumbling into the temple. Cast aside and crashing up against the wall, I watched as Jayda and Parlo, along with the three men and two ladies who had left the temple, came rushing inside toward the safety of the merkabah.

Jayda ran straight into Leesha's arms, to her relief. I could see his eyes familiarizing himself with the temple. Releasing Leesha, he turned to Benjamin. "Where is Nara?"

Benjamin pointed to me, my back pressed against the wall. "She will not come until everyone is returned, and yet the Celestial White Beings assure me they will return for the others." Devastation filled his voice.

"Where are Martyna and Ela?" I commanded Jayda to answer me.

"Nara, we couldn't find them," Jayda spoke gently.

"Then I must search for and find them." The determination in my voice revealed that there was no other option.

"Then I will come with you," Jayda announced.

"No!" Leesha, Benjamin, and I concurred.

"Jayda, you must go with the others. I will stay with Nara and search for Martyna and Ela." As Benjamin stepped out of the merkabah, as if it was meant to be, the merkabah and all our loved ones disappeared before our eyes. They were gone, safeguarded by the Celestial White Beings, and the temple was empty except for Benjamin and me. We stood awkwardly side by side, trying to comprehend what had just occurred.

"Nara, I understand why you have created this. You cannot leave your mother behind. I understand, but it doesn't mean I am happy about this situation. I know our egos, fears, and elements of drama are rising within us. I see this in all of us — a difficultly in remaining in love, our inner clarity disregarded — and it disappoints me. Nara, sometimes we just have to accept certain circumstances and let things be as they are meant to unfold." Benjamin radiated anger and despair. He turned away from me and stormed out through the temple door.

I did not care about Benjamin's feelings in that moment. Fear and my ego were taking a hold of me in a way I had never experienced before while creating a sense of courage. I pulled out my White Beacon to light my way as I moved through the temple door. The wild winds, darkness, toxic smell, and debris pounded my face and body, and I lost my confidence in finding Martyna and Ela. I became disoriented and collapsed onto my knees with the force of the wind. I searched with my white beacon, casting light on my surroundings. Nothing seemed familiar to me. Trees were broken and cast onto the land; buildings normally situated at the bottom of the hill leading to the temple were strewn all the way to the top. Sheltering my eyes from the flying debris and rain, I drew myself to my feet.

"Benjamin, where are you?" I yelled into the howling wind. There was no answer. "Benjamin, I am sorry. Please answer me. I do not recognize myself. Where are you?" I yelled with all my might.

"Nara, is that you?" I heard only a faint female whisper.

"Who is it? Where are you?" I questioned, searching violently with my white beacon, casting light all around me.

Again, there was no answer. I began to run to my left, believing that to be the direction of the voice, but it felt like the wind was playing tricks on me, coming at me from all directions and trying to toss me to the ground. Then I saw it: a delicate hand waving frantically from behind a large stone. The stone was embedded in a dip in the hillside, which was familiar to me. The dip was akin to a lower-level pathway that ran down the side of the entire hill. Lowering myself carefully onto the pathway, using the stone for support, I saw Martyna lying on her back. Pain, agony, and tears distorted her face. Carefully resting my white beacon wand on top of the stone to cast light on Martyna, I noticed that she was covered in mud as if she had tumbled down the hill. She clutched the top of her left leg.

"Oh, Nara, I am so grateful to see you. I am in such agony! I think I have broken my leg. The pain is excruciating. I was searching for Ela and lost my footing in the dark and started to tumble down the hill. My body crashed up against this stone, breaking my leg, I fear, in the process. I gradually maneuvered myself to this position to gain shelter from the stone. Have they been — the Celestial White Beings? Have I missed them? I heard Jayda and Parlo run by. I shouted to them, but they didn't hear me. I have been calling for Ela. I need assistance to move, though." Martyna spoke frantically. Her words were quick and agitated. She continued to chatter away, and once I freed her, she was still scared and in shock.

"Martyna, I want to take you back to the refuge of the temple. I am going to place my arms around you and lift you to your feet." I spoke calmly and clearly to my mother while I used all my strength to lift her body. I began a process of pulling her, dragging her, carrying her, and encouraging her to take small steps herself. Her body was just too heavy for me to assist her in the way I wished to. Finally, as Martyna realized what was happening, she began to hop on her healthy leg, using my body as support.

With effort, we made it through the temple doors where we both collapsed on the floor, breathless and weary. Delving deep within to connect with my inner strength, I pulled myself from the floor and maneuvered Martyna into the center of the temple in preparation for the return of the Celestial White Beings' merkabah. I placed a pillow under her head and a blanket over her shaking body. Kissing her on the forehead, I shared I would return; however, I needed to continue searching. I felt such guilt for leaving Martyna alone in the temple, yet I needed to find Benjamin and Ela.

This time I approached the unfamiliar outside world with caution, my footsteps tentative and my search with the light of the White Beacon firm and precise.

"Benjamin! Benjamin! Ela! Benjamin!" I shouted. This time, I walked toward my right side. I knew I was close to the clifftop where I often used to look out across the ocean. I wearily entered the forest area, stopping often to gaze in all directions. The rain was falling harder, and every so often I felt a heavy wall of water hit my body, knocking me forward with great force. I knew, like the weather, the ocean was becoming wild, throwing itself onto the land.

"Love sweeps like an ocean over and through Atlantis and its people. The love of the Creator is now our reality. All pain, suffering, and misalignment are erased eternally," I mumbled, trying to comfort myself as another sheet of salty water crashed up against me. "Like an ocean … over and through … misalignment is erased eternally … we have been creating a tidal wave … we have been creating the fall of Atlantis … it is all my fault … the Celestial White Beings have caused this … I trusted … oh, and Benjamin … I am sorry …" My mind was reeling with thoughts and realizations. I had so many questions, yet my only desire was to find Benjamin. I began to run as fast as I could, as if trying to flee my thoughts and realizations.

"Nara!" An excruciating yell entered my mind. I recognized the voice instantly: It was Benjamin. I stopped and turned slowly around, pausing for a moment to try to detect where Benjamin's voice was coming from. Then I realized Benjamin was speaking to me telepathically. His voice wasn't coming from outside of me; it was inside my mind. I stood still, gained my composure, and focused on my breathing. I saw at my third eye chakra a pure white light radiating into my mind and outward toward Benjamin. I felt we were connected, so I began a very calm conversation with him.

"Benjamin, is that you? Answer me," I telepathically transmitted.

After waiting a few moments and maintaining my focus, I heard a familiar voice respond: "Yes, Nara, it is Benjamin. Can you hear me?"

"Yes. Where are you, Benjamin? Tell me what has happened." I calmly projected.

"Oh, Nara, I am so thankful to connect with you. I am so sorry I deserted you and can't be there for you now. Please forgive me," Benjamin's projection continued, but he wasn't answering my questions.

With fear once more building within me, I called on the peace of my soul. "Again, Benjamin, where are you? Tell me what has happened," I projected so forcefully it seemed to cut through his chatter.

"Nara, I am at the bottom of the forest near the stream. Please come to me." Benjamin's words came with a picture projection akin to a map of precisely where he was.

I began to run in the darkness following Benjamin's guidance in my mind as he directed me through the trees. My White Beacon illuminated any fallen trees blocking my pathway. As I came to the familiar clearing, I ran farther down toward the stream. A white light was extending into the sky. It was Benjamin; he was using his beacon to help me find his position. As I drew closer, I saw the beacon was illuminating Benjamin as well. I registered he was lying down, and I collapsed down beside him. My arms cast across his torso as I squeezed him tightly to me.

"Agghh! Nara, stop!" Benjamin yelled.

Shocked by his response, I loosened by grip and opened my eyes. The vision I saw felt like it had torn my breath from my body. I tried to grasp my breath — to find it, catch, it or even return it to my body. I couldn't breathe through shock of seeing a shiny blade embedded in Benjamin's chest, as if right through his heart. My voice made recognizable sounds and yet my mind could not form any common sentence. Benjamin's large hand came up to gently brush my red hair aside and caress my face. I noticed his eyes were so beautiful and clear, and they focused on me.

"Nara, stay present with me. Stay in your center. All is well and as it should be." I could barely hear Benjamin's whisper as it competed with the worsening conditions around us.

"No, Benjamin, you cannot die. This cannot happen. You cannot leave me! This is not the way it is meant to be ...." My voice failed me.

"This is precisely the way it is meant to be, Nara. We are the creators of our reality, and some things are created by our souls that we cannot escape. I am going home, Nara, to the Celestial White Beings. It is wonderful. This is happening to make you strong. I am your strength, your protector. We are soul mates, and you have to find the energy you see in me in yourself. One of your greatest lessons is to master your emotions. You can let them flow freely while holding a strong sense of your power within. Have courage, Nara. I will always be with you," Benjamin shared with peace and joy.

Tears rolled down my face. "No, Benjamin. I don't want to be strong!" I argued.

"Nara, your soul has asked to experience this. Your soul loves you. I love you. You are safe," Benjamin reassured me. His hand slipped away from my face.

"Benjamin, how can I help you? How did this happen to you? What should I do?" I asked as I lowered my face to his so I could hear his quiet words of wisdom.

No words came. I realized Benjamin was no longer breathing. He had left his body. I felt hysteria rise in response to my reality as I slumped over him, crying tears of loss. My heart felt as if it was crumbling away, and my entire body grew numb. Emptiness and devastation tried to take over my body, mind, and emotions, but I felt shock and pain give way to a sense of deep-seated peace — as if Benjamin's peace had been passed on to me. I remembered Benjamin's words for me to be strong. He had wanted me to activate my inner strength and power and use them to yield love and to carve my truth into my reality.

"Go to the temple," my inner strength spoke to me.

I gazed at Benjamin. I wanted to imprint his image eternally into my mind. I kissed him lovingly, gently removed his beacon from his still warm hand, and unfastened the lapis lazuli crystal he always wore around his neck and placed it around my own. I took a few moments to bless his body and soul, affirming we would be together once more as soon as the divine Creator intended. It took all my willpower to stand up and walk away from Benjamin, leaving him lying there alone, yet a strong intuition was guiding me from within, telling me to have faith, to return to the temple, and most importantly, to remain connected to the well of strength within me. Even with my guiding knowingness, I gazed back at Benjamin every few steps, unable to truly grasp my unfolding reality.

After walking steadily and slowly up the hill, retracing my footsteps through the forest as best I could, I finally neared the temple. I felt battered and abused by the fierce conditions around me — completely drenched from head to toe by the rain and walls of sea water being thrown onto the land and disoriented by my changing surroundings as well as the constant tremor of the earth beneath me in the darkness. My outward suffering seemed like nothing compared to my inner feelings of pain, loss, and loneliness. With my face cast downward, I followed the light of the two White Beacons held in my hands as I made my way to the entrance of the temple. The light of my beacons began to illuminate rubble, rocks, and debris, which I picked my way through. As I stepped over a small white wall protruding from the debris, a horrifying realization struck my thoughts of pain and abandonment. I turned, scanning my surrounding with the two White Beacons. To my dismay, I realized I had reached my temple and had just stepped over its remaining foundations. The shaky light of my beacons illuminated a piece of the temple roof and its mammoth crystal shattered within the remaining temple walls, which at the tallest part were no higher than my head. My temple was gone — destroyed — and had fallen to the ground, its safety and security no longer available to me. I slumped down in despair, my back against a small remaining wall to shelter my weary body. Rubble and stones surrounded me, and all I knew was gone. All remains of hope and strength within me seemed to dissolve, leaving an empty space.

I wondered whether Martyna had been collected by the Celestial White Beings or was buried in the rubble beneath me. I couldn't bear to picture her face, to picture my family, friends, Benjamin, and all I had lost. It was too excruciating. I could feel my body and my senses begin to close down as if there was nothing on Atlantis to keep me present any longer. I began an internal conversation with myself and the inner strength that had guided me to this agonizing scene.

"Why did you guide me here? I don't understand. It's cruel to show me the fall of my temple when I could have remained close to Benjamin," I accused my inner guidance, wishing to cast blame to ease the pain that was tearing me apart.

There was no response.

"You are not so courageous now, are you? This is cruel. The Celestial White Beings are callous. I trusted them with all my heart." Anger began to rage within me.

"This is where you are meant to be. It is a place of tremendous energy and connection with the inner planes," my inner voice offered.

"I no longer believe. I no longer believe in you. I feel betrayed and abused." My anger continued to want to battle with anyone who would respond.

"You are not alone. Benjamin and the Celestial White Beings are here with you," my inner voice offered once more.

My surroundings seemed to dampen in sound and vision as a swirling white light moving around me attracted my attention.

"Nara, you are safe. I have you in my arms. Relax and let go. It is time." Benjamin's voice and love echoed through me. I could hear his familiar voice singing to me: "Although the wind, the wind will blow, let your light shine bright. Although the rain, the rain will fall, let your love shine bright. Although the storms, the storms will come, let your peace guide you home, for the sun, the sun will shine, and embrace you forever more." My anger softened. My entire being responded to Benjamin. My soul was now ready to leave the torment of my reality, and I obeyed. I let go with one single exhalation.

Nara's Notes

The fall of Atlantis was different for each of us. Every soul who incarnated on Atlantis will have their story to tell. Some stories may express feelings of loss, pain, grief, confusion, or regret while others may hold memories of feeling safe, supported, loved, and safeguarded. Every soul played its part in the fall of Atlantis; each soul created the fall of Atlantis for a reason, so blame is not an option. Yet there may be emotions experienced at the fall of Atlantis that you have held and carried through lifetimes, especially into your current lifetime. Now is the time for all of us to heal our wounds, emotions, memories, and stories of the fall of Atlantis so that we no longer consciously or unconsciously imprint patterns from Atlantis into our current experiences.

In many ways, our lifetimes are like plays staged in a theater. They feel real when we act them out, and we become very involved with our characters and the drama created. However, when the play is over, we return to the inner planes and can see the truth once more. When we return to Earth to act in a new play, we are reminded of the previous play, as its words, senses, and experiences are imprinted into the new play. The transition from being involved in a lifetime to seeing beyond its illusion, drama, and narrow-mindedness is beautiful. We are constantly in a process of experiencing it — even in everyday life. The imprinted patterns of the past are simply there to guide us and ensure further understanding or growth in new lifetimes. Often the lessons of one lifetime are resolved in another. With the quickening of ascension in your own reality, you no longer need to wait for your next lifetime; however, you are still resolving the lessons of your past lifetimes.

Whether you have been illuminated with insights of your Atlantean lifetime and your experiences during the fall of Atlantis or not, you can permit yourself to move through a process of release and healing to complete your Atlantean life in your current lifetime. This is essentially the purpose of our connection in this moment: By sharing my story, I am supporting the healing and completion of your own story, whether you are conscious or unconscious of this process. I cocreate with you a deep, meaningful healing and release of all unneeded energies that you may be holding on to consciously and unconsciously concerning the fall of Atlantis.

If your story is different from mine (although my story has not yet finished), it does not matter, because — remember — I am sharing my story through the perspective of my two eyes, seeing, sensing, and experiencing what I choose to focus on. For me, the fall of Atlantis activated and allowed me to experience fears of loss, separation, not being good enough, and abandonment, illuminating for me the need to access and cultivate my inner power. To overcome my fears, I simply needed to master my emotions, which means staying centered and grounded. I also needed to believe in my inner strength, putting into practice all that the Celestial White Beings had taught me. It is easy to remain in a space of love, truth, faith, and trust when in meditation, but you are completely challenged when in a hostile environment. I see the beauty in my reactions and their divine message from my inner knowingness to myself.

Benjamin and I were required to stay on Atlantis to complete the learning our souls wished to experience, causing everyone around us to cocreate the scenario for our learning to take place. There is no form of failure — only growth and further self-understanding. As Nara, I was supported so thoroughly by the Celestial White Beings, Jayda, Benjamin, Hamna, Amka, Martyna, Parlo, and so many more. I thank all souls for their constant support. My lesson of growth was to realize those who surrounded me were a reflection of my inner truth. I was given the opportunity to activate, experience, and exercise from within the qualities I admired in my loved ones. Whether I achieved and exercised this lesson does not matter, because the seed has been planted and will continue to grow.

Practice 32
The Meaning of the Fall of Atlantis

In our realities, we do not need to understand the meaning or purpose of circumstances. Acceptance and release are the sacred tools that command our focus; however, there is always an aspect of our being that wishes to understand every minute detail. I wish to offer you a space of understanding for your soul to choose, to grasp, and to inspire your mind — or not, whatever is divinely appropriate. This opportunity of further understanding I share with you now.

Take a moment to sit peacefully and enter a meditative state by focusing on your breathing. Say out loud,

I call on the divinely loving conscious source of sacred wisdom, knowledge, and remembrance of the Celestial White Being's soul group to manifest above my head in the shape of a pure white, pearlescent pyramid. The base of the pyramid rests within my crown chakra while the top of the pyramid rests within and encompasses my soul star chakra directly above my crown chakra. This symbolizes that the wisdom I receive is guided, inspired, and overseen by my soul. I am ready to receive the understanding that will divinely inspire and aid my spiritual evolution at this time of my ascension. I am open to receive and comprehend with ease and perfection. Thank you.

The Celestial White Beings surround you in a circle of white light. I invite you to breathe with your focus at your crown chakra. As you inhale, imagine the light and wisdom of the pyramid moving into your crown chakra. As you exhale, imagine, sense, or acknowledge the energy expanding into your head, mind, brain, and thoughts. Practice this until you can sense a heightened consciousness moving through your awareness.

You may wish to simply exist in this state, allowing any inspiration, insights, or guidance to dawn from the divinely loving conscious source of divine wisdom, knowledge, and remembrance of the Celestial White Beings' soul group. This energy, aligned with your soul, can illuminate your understanding tremendously. Trust will be required within your being and concerning your ability to receive wisdom. You may also wish to ask the questions below to guide any inspiration or necessary wisdom into fruition. Remember, your answers are personal to you, born from your own perspective now and during the time of Atlantis, guided by the expansive knowledge of your soul and the Celestial White Beings.

- *What was the meaning and purpose of the fall of Atlantis for me?*
- *What was the meaning and purpose of the fall of Atlantis for humanity?*
- *What cycles of growth born from Atlantis do I need to complete in my current reality?*

Practice 33
Cocreated Healing

Healing and releasing all energies, ties, imprinted patterns, belief systems, and illusions have been the purpose of my communication with you. Understanding information and knowledge is appropriate, but your experience of healing and releasing to make space for your greater volumes of love is essential and my key intention of connecting with you. I wish to guide you to cocreate healing for yourself, present-day humanity, and the Atlantean communities of present-day Atlantis. I invite you to allow yourself to be an instrument of the Celestial White Beings' cosmic healing vibrations to bring completion and healing to the cycle of Atlantis, dissolving all imprints from Atlantis in your modern day.

Sit peacefully and allow yourself to enter a space of meditation as you focus on your breathing. Say out loud,

I invoke my community of guides, my angelic guides, the protection of Archangel Michael, and the angels of Atlantis to surround and support me in their energy, light, healing, and love now. I am ready to receive healing and to facilitate healing where it is required. I open myself fully to receive and express healing. I invoke the Celestial White Beings' powerful pure healing vibrations to surround me and to collectively unite with the vibrations of my guides, my angelic guides, the protection of Archangel Michael, and the angels of Atlantis, pouring through my crown chakra and entire chakra column to be expressed as a vast beacon of healing light into the earth. Let these sacred healing vibrations be expressed from my heart in all directions. I am a beacon of healing light.

My purpose in this moment is to experience complete healing within my being, dissolving and letting go with ease and perfection all aspects within myself that hinder my expansion and spiritual evolution, especially in connection to Atlantis and its fall.

My purpose in this moment is to heal all souls who are and have been in existence on Atlantis. May they let go of all pain, suffering, blockages, and unneeded patterns and imprints of the mind and emotions, allowing for complete and absolute healing to take place within their beings.

My purpose in this moment is to send supreme healing to all souls present on Earth now who have been in existence on Atlantis and who are influencing our current ascension process in negative or limiting ways due to fear, pain, suffering, or illusions.

Let my healing vibrations support Mother Earth by bringing forth balance — especially between technology and the truth of the soul — as well as completing and erasing the purpose of Atlantis in positive, loving ways in our current reality. Thank you.

Allow yourself to take time to imagine healing light flowing from your being into the earth, humanity, and all the souls of Atlantis.

I, Nara, wish to thank you personally for being of service. Your healing is received with gratitude and is influencing the ascension of all. Please practice this process as often as you feel guided to do so.

16

The Truth

I felt deeply supported as I drifted in a river of love, ecstasy, and fulfillment. My entire being felt alive, rejuvenated, and pleasantly familiar. As I became consciously aware, my love vibrations heightened and overflowed from my being. My awareness brought me to a space of brilliant white light. Once I had integrated with my surroundings, I was greeted by the Celestial White Beings, who had gathered in a translucent ring of white light around me. Their tall lightbodies bobbed gently and radiated such blissful love that focused completely on me. I recognized the pure white chamber that encapsulated me as the healing and integration chamber of the Celestial White Beings at their home on the inner planes. I gazed down at my body and was surprised and somewhat relieved to see my white translucent lightbody rather than the physical manifestation and body of Nara. I felt free and able to be as my truth, recognizing myself as a Celestial White Being.

"You are now returned to us. We are one, beloved OmNa," they collectively transmitted to me. "It is important you take time to adjust. You still hold your memories as Nara because we will soon transport you to Egypt, manifesting you once more from light into a new adult physical body, which will resemble your previous body. This means your earthly perspectives remain with you and are essential for your return to Earth. Your consciousness will expand as you exist in your lightbody now so that greater understanding will flow to you. We have returned you to your home on the inner planes to prepare you for your community in Egypt, and there is much we wish to share with you."

"I am very happy to be with you, Celestial White Beings. To remember my oneness and complete integration with you, to remember my self and truth — it is such a relief. I did so enjoy my time on Earth as Nara. I collected and absorbed much to share with you. My soul is in complete bliss due to every single experience on Earth. It is fun to be on Earth, to be involved in one's self and create all forms of experiences. Such a blessing, such an honor." I transmitted all my blissful thoughts and feelings to the Celestial White Beings.

"We are already integrating with your light and receiving all that is appropriate from your lifetime. We love you deeply and are elated by all of your experiences on Earth." Love emanated from the Celestial White Beings.

I began to think of my experiences as Nara on Earth — memories of my childhood, of my temple, of communing with the Celestial White Beings, of Benjamin and my family. There was an air of detachment, and yet it still struck me — a feeling of discomfort as my memory raced through the latter experiences of my life.

"OmNa, be gentle with yourself. Remember you are still connected to Earth. Those ties and your ties to Nara have not been dissolved as they usually are when you fully return to the inner planes. We wish for you to maintain your connection with that aspect of yourself, so you might feel as if you exist between worlds until we return you to Egypt," the Celestial White Beings telepathically transmitted with such warm and tender love.

"Yes, I understand. Please share with me all you wish to. I do wish to embody a greater perspective of my reality as Nara."

I readied myself for a download of light, consciousness, and illumination. A brilliant white source of light moved into my conscious awareness, and it felt like the vibration of freedom. My entire being expanded as a deep-seated knowingness emerged. Allowing myself to surrender to the light, I was instantly fulfilled with deep-rooted understanding, as if the knowledge I was becoming aware of had always been present within me; I had simply been blind to it. I now understood the larger picture and divine plan for my entire existence as Nara.

"There is a soul who wishes to connect with you. We wish to now transport you to an ashram at the planetary level, the synthesis chamber within the Second Ray of Light Ashram representing a space and expression of love and wisdom from the Creator." The Celestial White Beings drew their light closer to me, becoming one with my energy.

My awareness brought me to the synthesis chamber and to a space I was familiar with. I was in a garden filled with shades of beautiful multicolored flowers and plants, glistening and shimmering with life force energy. My senses filled with color, splendor, and vibrancy. I sat on my favorite crystalline bench and allowed myself to inhale the breathtaking vibrations surrounding me. The

garden, I knew, was a picture and projection cocreated by my soul and the energies of the synthesis chamber — much like a tool to support my easy absorption
of the synthesis vibrations. The Celestial White Beings surrounded me in a circle
once more, their support flowing to me continuously.

"We have anchored your vibrations into the synthesis chamber to begin your
transformation and integration into your physical body. You will notice your
white lightbody is being overridden now by a light projection of your physical
body as Nara. This is a new process for you, as in all your lifetimes on Earth you
have been born as a baby. This time you will manifest as your adult Nara-self on
Earth, as if out of the air. We are lowering your energetic vibration so that you
can manifest as physical matter. For the first few days of your existence on Earth
and with your community, you will appear to them as a hologram until you fully
ground yourself into Mother Earth. You will not be alone on this new journey."
The Celestial White Beings' flow was interrupted by my squeal of joy.

"OmSe Na! Benjamin!" I shouted with ecstasy as I jumped from my seat.

I spotted OmSe Na walking toward me through the synthesis chamber garden. He looked exactly like Benjamin — tall and handsome; brown, shoulder-
length hair tied back; and dressed in pale-blue-and-white robes that illuminated
his sparkling eyes. Happiness and joy exuded from his being, which he extended
into the depths of my soul. A vibration of oneness ignited within me in response
to OmSe Na's connection.

"Nara! OmNa! My sacred soul mate!" Benjamin wrapped his lightbody arms
around me.

His embrace felt blissful and fulfilling. I recognized this was not due to his
physical presence and closeness that I had been accustomed to on Earth; he was
in his lightbody, projecting the image of the physical body I knew as Benjamin in
preparation for his return to Earth. Our light synthesis and merging felt enjoy-
able and satisfying. We continued to embrace each other as we sat down, and I
could feel a deeper connection with my emotions and thoughts as Nara while
the synthesis organized by the Celestial White Beings continued to prepare me
for my embodiment. With each moment, I was becoming more like Nara just as
OmSe Na was becoming more like Benjamin.

"OmSe Na, Benjamin, have you received enlightenment from the Celestial
White Beings?" I asked, feeling our energy and souls communicating beyond my
more mental transmission.

"Yes, I have received enlightenment for my existence. Not for yours, though,"
he responded.

"I realize now it is the same for me," I uttered as my memories began to appear once more, flashing through my mind. The synthesis enhanced, causing us to see and sense ourselves and each other in our earthly aspects.

"Please forgive me for walking out and leaving you in the temple alone, Nara. Forgive me for not being with you physically at the end, for not being there to support and protect you as is my purpose." Pain flashed across Benjamin's face as he remembered his experiences.

"Benjamin, this is your personality speaking. You know I forgive you. It was all divinely planned. We were creating scenarios of growth for each other, and it was fun to experience." I noticed Benjamin's inner glow returning with the truth of my words. "Why were you lying on the ground with a knife in your chest? How did that happen?"

"Ah, yes. Well, I managed to find Ela with the light of my beacon. She was crouched down against a rock beside the stream, so I shouted to her as I made my way closer. However, the noise of the wind was so loud that my voice was lost. When I reached her, I realized she was sinking into thoughts of fear. Her fear was engulfing her. Even as I stood before her, she did not respond to my words, so I gently placed my hands on her arms to lift her to her feet. This shocked her from her thoughts of fear, making her aware of my presence. I didn't realize she had been holding a knife. She sank the knife into my chest. The pain shocked me, and I fell backward. Nara, it was like time disappeared. I felt I was falling to the ground for such a long time with excruciating pain smothering my chest, and that's when I shouted for you. It suddenly dawned on me I had left you alone; the realization was more painful than the embedded knife.

"Nara, the Celestial White Beings came to me and filled me with peace, which I was grateful to be able to share with you. I had a profound knowingness that all was well, and of course it was." Benjamin smiled.

"How did the Celestial White Beings come to you?"

"The same way I came to you when you were ready to leave Atlantis — they connected with my soul and channeled their energy and consciousness through my soul. They were not present with me as we know them to be in the temple; however, the connection was stronger than I had previously experienced. I feel that this will be the new way we will all connect with and experience the Celestial White Beings in Egypt — personally, within our beings, as they channel their light through each of us. It dissolves all perceptions of separation." Benjamin was elated with his insight.

"And our community — they made it safely to Egypt?" I asked the Celestial White Beings, their energy beaming at me from all directions.

Their collective consciousness spoke into our minds: "Everyone was transported to this same ashram for renewal — to access illumination and to prepare for their new journey on Earth. They are now building a new life on Earth together. They know you both will return to them soon."

"And my Mother, Martyna? What happened to her? What about our baby? Will she be born through me in Egypt too?" I was anxious to know of their safety.

"Martyna's soul wished to experience the death of her physical body as a process of detachment and ascension. This was one of the greatest purposes of her soul for her lifetime. She was crushed by the falling debris of the temple created by earth tremors. She passed quickly into the inner planes with very little pain or suffering. Her soul has decided to continue to work with the community, so she has to experience that which you are now experiencing: the manifestation of yourself as light into a physical adult form on Earth.

"As for the sacred soul born into you, she will not return with you to Egypt. Her soul wanted to experience all you experienced in Atlantis as a sort of observer; it was never the soul's intention to be physically born on Atlantis. She will return and be born through you once more in another of your lifetimes. You will recognize her. All is well, Nara. Everything is unfolding beautifully as guided by the divine," the Celestial White Beings concluded.

"Thank you. I am grateful to know. I understand — through my death and the pain, dismay, and heartbreak I experienced at the end — that it is all a game of learning. It seems so real when you are present in its core, but now I truly acknowledge the treasure I have received from such an experience. I know it is the same for my mother." Gratitude tingled throughout my entire being, and I felt as if I were special to and cared for by the Creator.

"I too understand the rewards of such experiences; however, I believe there will come a time on Earth when our consciousnesses will be heightened and our souls will grow through miraculous experiences of love rather than pain and suffering. Nara, I truly feel enlightened. I feel that if you asked me any question, I would have the knowledge to answer you from the treasured wisdom within my source." Benjamin laughed, yet he knew he spoke the truth.

"Nara's pain still remains with me," I confided to Om Se Na. "Her guilt for not safeguarding the community as she would have wished to, her resentment toward the Celestial White Beings for tricking the community into creating the fall of Atlantis, and her pain for loosing you, Benjamin. I strongly feel her loneliness."

"OmNa, I am aware of similar energies held on to by my personality, Benjamin. We will bring deep healing and understanding to the personalities of Nara and Benjamin when we are on Earth. This can only be healed in the physical levels, due to their being born from those levels of understanding. We will heal ourselves," Benjamin gently reassured me.

"And what of Atlantis, our sacred land? What was really happening?" Again, I questioned the Celestial White Beings. I required clarity to carry understanding to my community on my return.

"Atlantis has fallen. Its land fragmented and submerged. This situation has affected the entire Earth. We are truly blessed, as many star civilizations stepped forth with their energy, light, consciousness, and technology to restore and save the planet from complete destruction. Atlantis is no longer. It is now the core of Earth's South Pole. When the magnetic fields of Earth were restored by the star civilizations, the planet went into a period of darkness that lasted many days. Countless people died, leaving their earthly reality and bodies behind. Those who survived have had their memories completely erased due to the magnetic pole shift. They will not remember this time unless their souls choose to speak to them and remind them. The people of Earth have been seeded with a new consciousness since the time of darkness ended and the sun returned once more. Your community was held in a transitional stage between Earth and the inner planes during the time of the pole shift, so their memories will remain with them."

"Who were the star civilizations supporting Earth?" Benjamin pressed.

"The Andromedans played a powerful role in the survival of Earth and suppressed many devastating reactions that could have occurred," the Celestial White Beings offered. It was the only information they could share.

"Wonderful!" Benjamin gasped in awe, satisfied with the answer.

"What of Earth?" I inquired, eager for more information and understanding.

"Earth has fallen in dimensions and now vibrates collectively at a slower rate. It may take humanity several civilizations and generations to return Earth to the quick vibration you are accustomed to that is more aligned with your souls.

"As you know, the vortex became smaller. You experienced the high winds and, of course, the tidal wave submerging Atlantis completely. This tidal wave came, OmNa, just after OmSe Na encouraged you to leave your body and return to the inner planes. We shared with you a mantra: 'Love sweeps like an ocean over and through Atlantis and its people. The love of the Creator is now our reality. All pain, suffering, and misalignment are erased eternally.' We knew Atlantis couldn't survive. To save Earth, Atlantis needed to be terminated. This creation also needed to be requested by those on Earth, such as your community. That is why we shared the mantra with you. Your soul had already consented; we did not deceive you. We also encouraged you to visit central Atlantis so that the mantra could be embedded within the consciousnesses of the priests and priestesses without their awareness and they would create the same. It truly was an act of love that we all created for the future ascension of Earth and humanity. Chaos can sometimes be created from love to bring forth transformation and a new beginning."

"Has the purpose of Atlantis been fulfilled?" Benjamin asked, seemingly plucking the words from my mind.

"The purpose of Atlantis and its civilizations at its creation was to experience balance between the masculine and feminine vibrations of the Creator through the process of exploring the inner spiritual and outer journeys, resulting in exploration, new understanding, and balance. As machines began to manifest to support physical reality and spiritual evolution, the inner spiritual journey was lost and became unimportant to many. Humanity was asked to live as their spiritual divine selves in a physical world and to live in balance with technology, which is to use technology from a space of truth within the self rather than allowing the self to be carried away from truth. Yet this only seemed to lead to destruction, which cannot be sustained. The divine will of the Creator needed to be brought forth to create balance once more.

"Atlantis was an experiment that has offered meaningful insights and knowledge, and the destruction must come to an end to allow new beginnings. There will come a time on Earth when Atlanteans will return simultaneously to Earth and complete the purpose of Atlantis, existing and encouraging others to exist as their divine selves in a physical reality in harmony with machines, technology, and inner spiritual discovery, thus manifesting the Creator and heaven on Earth through each soul present.

"It is now time for you, OmNa and OmSe Na, to return to Earth, to your community, and to your new reality. We will continue to be present with you, journeying with you always," the Celestial White Beings lovingly shared.

Our surroundings blurred as our awareness moved through light dimensions, downloading our consciousness into matter.

My only feelings were of excitement and pure joy. "I can't wait to begin another journey with you, Benjamin and the Celestial White Beings!"

Nara's Notes

We returned to Egypt to be greeted by our community and family. Our reunion was one of gratitude, happiness, and wonder. Although I was the same soul and in a body that was identical to my previous body, I knew I was to be different. New aspects of my soul had anchored into my Egyptian lifetime to assist my journey, and I had been transformed by my experiences in Atlantis. I share this with you to support your realization that we are the same as we move through our lifetimes; however, we are also diverse and different because we channel different aspects of our souls, depending on what is needed during the lifetime. Through sharing in my experiences and memories of my Atlantean lifetime, you have supported my growth and exploration of myself and enhanced my spiritual maturity. By simply sharing with you, I have collected knowledge to give back to the universe and my soul group. When you share your truth on Earth, you will move through renewed processes of collecting and engaging with yourself and truth.

I have shared with you only a small portion of my experiences and lifetime in Atlantis, including the amazing people I connected with and the insight I collected. I have shared only necessary information to inspire you as an Atlantean returning to Earth to share your truth, wise consciousness, keys, and tools.

Proudly stand on Earth knowing you are present with a great force of light that supports you with the power to transform yourself and the world to complete the original purpose and mission of Atlantis. You have the support of Benjamin, me, the Celestial White Beings, the angels of Atlantis, the ascended masters, and the archangels. I, Nara, made a contract to continue to support your spiritual evolution and ascension. I achieve this from the inner planes energetically and through my soul's current embodiment as Natalie. Her physical writing of this book brings forth a completion of cycles for my soul and yours.

You are never alone as you journey. You are your soul, connected to all things — here to bring peace, love, harmony, and balance to Earth; here to enhance your connection and the alignment of all with the Creator. You are extremely loved and valued. You have always been and will continue to be guided if you are willing to listen and accept from within your being. The return of Atlantis is here, and the dawning of the completion of Atlantis rises through you.

I have one final practice I wish to share with you to empower you as you move to the next stage of your spiritual evolution. It has been an honor to share with you.

Practice 34
Empowerment

You may wish to say this invocation out loud. Then simply sit, breathe in deeply, and receive the blessings showering over and on you as well as igniting from within you.

I call forth all the loving, sacred energies of Atlantis to flow through my being. I choose to receive the sacred consciousness, healing, sound frequencies, wisdom, crystalline vibrations, and codes of awakening from Atlantis that are relevant in empowering my current ascension process. May the energies of Atlantis empower, balance, heal, awaken, rejuvenate, inspire, sustain, and bring greater peace to my being, humanity, and Earth.

I am ready to receive my true self. I am ready to be my truth. I am ready to share my truth. I Am That I Am; I am the truth of the Creator. I am present now for a reason that I am fulfilling with every moment of my day. May my sacred Atlantean connections, roots, abilities, and love eternally walk with me, positively inspiring and empowering my ascension on Earth. Let it be so.

With all my love and support,
Nara

Glossary

angel. A being of light created from the heart and love energy of the Creator. Angels act as messengers from the Creator to humanity and hold all loving qualities of the Creator for humanity to absorb and embody. We can call on the angels to assist us in all matters within our reality and spiritual growth because they will align us to the core and essential energy of the Creator.

archangel. A being that holds the same purpose as an angel but also oversees the work and purpose of an angelic kingdom or community. Archangels could be seen as the leaders and essential holders of important Creator energies and qualities for humanity to absorb and embody. They are powerhouses of love that divinely intervene in our realities when we ask and allow them to.

Archangel Michael. Known as an overseer of all angels of protection, Archangel Michael supports the manifestation of the divine will of the Creator while acting as a great source of protection to call on in your everyday life.

ascended master. A soul that has existed on Earth and has realized him- or herself as truth and as the Creator. An ascended master has disciplined and brought into balance his or her emotions, thoughts, and energy bodies to exist in harmony and peace with the Creator and all that is the Creator. Ascended masters hold a great volume of knowledge and act as guides to humanity from the spiritual levels and planes. With the current changes that are occurring, more ascended masters are choosing to delay their ascension because they wish to assist humanity.

ascension. The process of self-realization, soul realization, and Creator realization. It is a period of growth when one focuses on aligning to the Creator's soul and becoming the Creator. Ascension is the journey of evolvement you walk from the moment of your awakening to the moment of complete alignment with the Creator.

ashram. A sacred space that can be created on Earth or the inner planes where one can align to divine energies and learn or practice specific teachings to aid growth.

aura/auric field. Numerous energy bodies that extend from the physical body and chakras to create a large energy light form around a person expressing his or her consciousness, thoughts, and emotions as well as retaining knowledge and wisdom. The aura demonstrates more of a person's truth and soul than the physical body.

Celestial White Beings. A soul group that exists from the fourteenth dimension onward. They supported the creation of Earth to aid humanity's ascension. Their presence is formless and nameless, existing only as pure white light, although they present themselves in different forms to aid our acceptance. They are one source of light, even though they show themselves as many beings.

chakras. Energy points, wheels, or vortexes within our physical and energetic bodies that hold and absorb the Creator's light. They maintain our perfect health and well-being on a spiritual and physical level by ensuring a constant flow of life force energy around our bodies. They are arranged as follows: the earth star chakra below the feet, the root chakra at the base of the spine, the sacral chakra below the waist, the solar plexus chakra above the waist, the heart chakra at the chest center, the throat chakra at the throat, the third eye chakra at the brow, the crown chakra at the top of the head, and the soul star chakra above the head.

channel. Can be thought of as an invisible tube built into the crown chakra that extends into the heavens. The channel is built from light and allows light, energy, and wisdom to enter the human mind, body, and reality.

consciousness. A state of awareness, perception, understanding, realization, knowledge, and active presence, often aligned with the Creator.

Creator. One of the many names for God, the Source, the Universe, or the Divine.

crystalline being/kingdom. Physical crystals found on Earth have spirits or energy within their earthly form born from the inner planes. A crystalline being extends from the crystalline kingdom and is a soul and consciousness in existence beyond Earth. Crystalline vibrations are immensely purifying, uplifting, and supportive when received within the physical body.

crystal singing bowls. Musical instruments formed in the shape of a bowl that are made from crystal. Crystal singing bowls emanate healing frequencies while often being aligned to the sound of a chakra. The sound penetrates the cells of the physical body, aligning and balancing all cells to bring rejuvenation, healing, and heightened states of spiritual awareness.

ego. The aspect of self that believes in and creates from illusion. The positive purpose of the ego is to protect, but when given too much power, it can create limiting illusions such as fear, doubt, disbelief, and anxiety as well as a perception of separation from the Creator.

elementals. Spirits and souls existing on an unseen level who devote their energy and purpose to caring for and nurturing the earth, nature kingdoms, and Mother Earth.

dimensions. The space where the ascended masters, angels, and all lightbeings exist. Also known as the inner planes, the heavens, or unseen levels of energy beyond Earth's.

divine relationship. A soul connection relationship in which each person recognizes the truth of the Creator within his or her own being and the other and shares and interacts with this understanding. A divine relationship can enhance the ascension of both people because they focus on synthesizing their energies with the Creator through their interaction.

fairies. Souls who devote their energy and purpose to working alongside nature and the animal kingdom to allow the Creator's energy to anchor, blossom, and thrive. People who work closely with Mother Earth often have fairy guides who are pure loving beings of light holding the ancient knowledge of how to exist as one with Mother Earth.

goddess. A being of light who holds the feminine, nurturing, and creative qualities, energy, and wisdom of the Creator.

guides. Most often refers to those who assist us on an unseen level, supporting or inspiring our spiritual growth. We each have a special community of guides who surround us and assist us in our everyday reality, especially when we allow them to. These guides are most often beings with whom we have held a strong connection in the past or who hold wisdom that is essential for our growth.

healing. A process of restoring balance, well-being, and happiness to the physical, mental, emotional, and spiritual aspects of being. Through healing, we experience a deepening resonance with the Creator as a reflection of the divine Source.

inner planes. The unseen levels of energy beyond Earth's physical and heavy vibration. These are the dimensions or heavens of the Creator, the space where the ascended masters, angels, and all lightbeings exist.

initiations. Cycles, processes, journeys, or practices that promote awakening, acceptance of one's true self, and an accelerated embodiment of light.

intuition. The instinct, insight, and knowing feeling within you that acts as a guiding light along your path. Everyone has the ability to use their intuition. To follow your intuition is to follow your soul and Creator wisdom.

Kuthumi, Master. An ascended master who has moved through numerous lifetimes on Earth, such as Saint Frances of Assisi and Pythagoras, to exist on the inner planes as a world teacher alongside Master Sananda (Jesus). Before accepting his role as overseer of the spiritual education of humanity, Master Kuthumi supervised the Second Ray of Light of love and wisdom.

life force energy. The vibrational flow of energy and creation from the Creator. It gives life, nourishment, and sustenance to all forms of manifestations.

lightbeing. A soul, person, essence, or energy that holds and emanates the light of the Creator.

lightbody. A sacred grid of light that awakens from the auric field with spiritual development to aid ascension. It houses your soul when you evolve from your physical existence and when you travel to ashrams on the inner planes during your sleep state.

light quotient. The volume or percentage of light or Creator energy that you hold within your mind and body.

light language. The language and communication of the vibrational light of the inner planes, heavens, ascended masters, archangels, and angels.

manifestation. The fine-tuning and projection of the mind and emotions into your reality to experience your wants and desires.

mantra. Words or sounds repeated either verbally or within the mind to bring focus, peace, healing, and harmony to the entire being. A mantra can also be an affirmation that states you have or already are that which you wish to be, therefore projecting positive, fulfilling experiences into your reality.

meditation. A practice to encourage us to connect with the energy of peace and harmony within us, dissolving all thoughts and simply existing in the present moment to observe ourselves and our energies. Meditation disciplines the mind and creates a stillness that awakens the senses, thus creating or developing new spiritual connections.

Melchizedek. A consciousness and source on the inner planes overseeing the universal level of the Creator's dimensions. Those of the Order of Melchizedek study, hold, and bring forth the wisdom and knowledge from this source. Melchizedek is a great foundation of light, wisdom, and healing that anyone can call on for support and guidance.

merkabah. A living light vehicle or electromagnetic field situated around the body like a three-dimensional geometric web that can be activated for traveling or shifting to different aspects of reality and dimensions of light. Each person has his or her own merkabah, which can be activated and retains valuable wisdom.

Mother Earth. The divine feminine essence and spirit of Earth and the nature kingdom.

portal. An opening, entrance, or gateway connecting worlds or realities through which energy and light waves flow.

soul. The essence and truth of your being. Your soul is the aspect, energy, light, love, and knowledge within you that originally extended from your soul group, which is an extension of the Creator's soul. Your soul is your Creator presence.

soul group. An original extension of light and consciousness from the Creator that then creates twelve extensions known as souls. Your soul is one of twelve extensions from your soul group. From your soul, there are an additional twelve extensions, of which your manifestation on Earth is one. Soul extensions can exist on Earth or the inner planes.

soul sounding. To express a vibration of sound from your voice or a musical instrument that aligns with, resonates with, or carries the essence of your soul into your physical reality.

soul symbol. A symbol that describes, aids connection, or resonates with your soul's energy, purpose, light, or wisdom. It can act as a representation of your soul and is often used for meditation.

spirit. A word often used to depict a soul or the essence of a person. It can also be used to describe a person who exists without a physical body. The spirit of a person is her or his divine will, determination, intuition, creativity, and strength — essentially, that person's entire energy.

telepathic communication. The ability to communicate or receive words, ideas, and feelings without the use of speech, writing, or normal signaling.

tree spirit. The soul, essence, or consciousness that inhabits and protects a tree.

unicorn. A being of pristine light that has the same energy vibration as the angelic kingdom. Often seen as ascended horses, unicorns hold a powerful ability to aid and teach manifestation as well as create miracles in your reality. They are powerful healers holding the energy of purity.

About the Author

NATALIE SIAN GLASSON is a channel, author, workshop facilitator, spiritual mentor, and the founder of the Sacred School of OmNa. She has been a channel for more than ten years, dedicating her life to assisting others in awakening to the light of the Creator. Natalie has always been able to connect with and express the consciousness of numerous ascended masters, archangels, angels, elementals, goddess beings, and star beings. She shares new wisdom and enlightenment to aid emergence of the divine energy within the physical body, thus supporting the manifestation the era of love.

Natalie is known for her powerful channeling abilities, and the Creator's love and the manifestation of inner bliss are at the center of her communications. Natalie's soul extends from the Celestial White Beings, and she is currently acting as a representative of their energy and consciousness on Earth.

Natalie's first book, *Twelve Rays of Light: A Guide to the Rays of Light and the Spiritual Hierarchy,* was published in the UK in 2010 and was later translated into the Lithuanian. Natalie facilitates channeled workshops in London, Glastonbury, Ireland, Wales, and Lithuania. Through the Sacred School of OmNa, she also shares a free weekly channeled message, meditation downloads, webinars, and much more to inspire personal exploration and ascension.

Natalie made a contract many lifetimes ago during the time of Atlantis to be of service. She continues to assist people in anchoring into their bodies the sacred energies available in the universe, as light, love, and consciousness are the keys to spiritual development. In her spare time, she enjoys focusing on her own spiritual awakening, playing her crystal singing bowls, painting, and practicing kundalini yoga. Born and brought up in Wales, Natalie now lives in London. For more information about her and her work, visit www.OmNa.org.

☀ *Light Technology* PUBLISHING *Presents*

THROUGH ROBERT SHAPIRO

Shamanic Secrets Mastery Series

Speaks of Many Truths, Zoosh and Reveals the Mysteries through Robert Shapiro

This book explores the heart and soul connection between humans and Earth. Through that intimacy, miracles of healing and expanded awareness can flourish. To heal the planet and be healed as well, you can lovingly extend your energy self out to the mountains and rivers and intimately bond with Earth. Gestures and vision can activate your heart to return you to a healthy, caring relationship with the land you live on. The character of some of Earth's most powerful features is explored and understood with exercises given to connect you with those places. As you project your love and healing energy there, you help Earth to heal from human destruction of the planet and its atmosphere. Dozens of photographs, maps, and drawings assist the process in twenty-five chapters, which cover Earth's more critical locations.

SOFTCOVER • 512 PP. • $19.95 • ISBN 978-1-891824-12-8

Learn to understand the sacred nature of your physical body and some of the magnificent gifts it offers you. When you work with your physical body in these new ways, you will discover not only its sacredness but also how it is compatible with Mother Earth, the animals, the plants, and even the nearby planets, all of which you now recognize as being sacred in nature. It is important to feel the value of oneself physically before you can have any lasting physical impact on the world. If a physical energy does not feel good about itself, it will usually be resolved; other physical or spiritual energies will dissolve it because they are unnatural. The better you feel about your physical self when you do the work in the first book, as well as this one and the one to follow, the greater and more lasting the benevolent effect will be on your life, on the lives of those around you, and ultimately on your planet and universe.

SOFTCOVER • 576 PP. • $25.00 • ISBN 978-1-891824-29-6

Spiritual mastery encompasses many different means to assimilate and be assimilated by the wisdom, feelings, flow, warmth, function, and application of all beings in your world that you will actually contact in some way. A lot of spiritual mastery has been covered in different bits and pieces throughout all the books we've done. My approach to spiritual mastery, though, will be as grounded as possible in things that people on Earth can use — but it won't include the broad spectrum of spiritual mastery, like levitation and invisibility. My life is basically going to represent your needs, and in a storylike fashion it gets out the secrets that have been held back." — Speaks of Many Truths

SOFTCOVER • 676 PP. • $29.95 • ISBN 978-1-891824-58-6

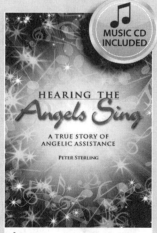

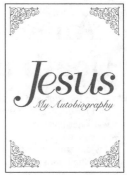
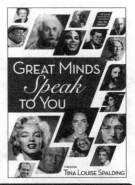

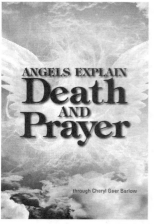

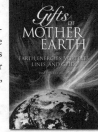

ᘰ *Light Technology* PUBLISHING *Presents*

TO ORDER PRINT BOOKS
Visit LightTechnology.com, Call 928-526-1345 or 1-800-450-0985,
or Check Amazon.com or Your Favorite Bookstore

THROUGH TOM T. MOORE

THE GENTLE WAY

A SELF-HELP GUIDE FOR THOSE WHO BELIEVE IN ANGELS

This book will put you back in touch with your guardian angel or strengthen and expand the connection that you already have. How can I promise these benefits? Because I have been using these concepts for years and I can report these successes from direct knowledge and experience.

$14.⁹⁵ • 160 PP., SOFTCOVER • ISBN 978-1-891824-60-9

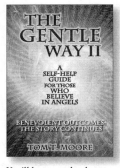

THE GENTLE WAY II

BENEVOLENT OUTCOMES: THE STORY CONTINUES

You'll be amazed at how easy it is to be in touch with guardian angels and how much assistance you can receive simply by asking. This inspirational self-help book, written for all faiths and beliefs, will explain how there is a more benevolent world that we can access and how we can achieve this.

$16.⁹⁵ • 320 PP., SOFTCOVER • ISBN 978-1-891824-80-7

THE GENTLE WAY III

MASTER YOUR LIFE

I continue to receive truly unique stories from people all over the world requesting most benevolent outcomes and asking for benevolent prayers for their families, friends, other people, and other beings. It just proves that there are no limits to this modality, which is becoming a gentle movement as people discover how much better their lives are with these simple yet powerful requests.

$16.⁹⁵ • 352 PP., SOFTCOVER • ISBN 978-1-62233-005-8

FIRST CONTACT

CONVERSATIONS WITH AN ET

This book contains vital information about our past, present, and future contact with ETs. Tom relays this information through conversations with "his brother from another planet," Antura.

$15.⁹⁵ • 224 PP., SOFTCOVER • ISBN 978-1-62233-004-1

ATLANTIS & LEMURIA

THE LOST CONTINENTS REVEALED!

Sixty thousand years ago, Earth had two more continents than it does today, each larger than what we now know as Australia. Why are they no longer there?

$16.⁹⁵ • 256 PP., SOFTCOVER • ISBN 978-1-62233-037-9

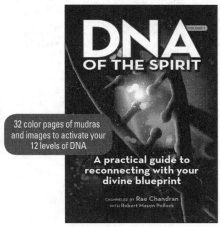

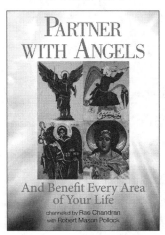
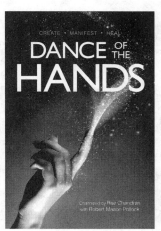

♃ *Light Technology* PUBLISHING *Presents*

THROUGH DAVID K. MILLER

Arcturians: How to Heal, Ascend, and Help Planet Earth

Go on a mind-expanding journey to explore new spiritual tools for dealing with our planetary crisis. Included in this book are new and updated interpretations of the Kaballistic Tree of Life, which has now been expanded to embrace fifth-dimensional planetary healing methods. Learn new and expanded Arcturian spiritual technologies.

$16.95 • 352 PP. • Softcover • 978-1-62233-002-7

Kaballah and the Ascension

"Throughout Western history, channeling has come to us in various forms, including mediumship, shamanism, fortunetelling, visionaries, and oracles. There is also a long history of channeling in Kaballah, the major branch of Jewish mysticism. I am intrigued by this, especially because I believe that there is now an urgent necessity for entering higher realms with our consciousness because of the impending changes on the planet. Through these higher realms, new healing energies and insights can be brought down to assist us in these coming Earth changes." — David K. Miller

$16.95 • 176 PP. • Softcover • 978-1-891824-82-1

Biorelativity: Planetary Healing Technologies

Biorelativity describes the ability of human beings to telepathically communicate with the spirit of Earth. The goal of such communication is to influence the outcome of natural Earth events such as storms, volcanic eruptions, and earthquakes. Through the lessons contained in this book, you can implement new planetary healing techniques right now, actively participating in exciting changes as Earth and humanity come together in unity and healing.

$16.95 • 352 PP. • Softcover • 978-1-891824-98-2

A New Tree of Life for Planetary Ascension

This is the second book David Miller has written about the Kabbalah. His first book, Kaballah and the Ascension, introduced basic concepts in the Kaballah and linked them to the ascended masters and the process of ascension. In this second book, David has teamed up with Torah scholar and Kabbalist expert Mordechai Yashin, who resides in Jerusalem, Israel. This book is based on unique lectures and classes David and Mordechai gave over an eight-month period between 2012 and 2013. These lectures on Jewish and Hebraic lessons were held in open discussion groups and offer a truly unique perspective into the Kabbalistic Tree of Life and how it has been expanded.

$16.95 • 464 PP. • Softcover • 978-1-62233-012-6

Raising the Spiritual Light Quotient

The spiritual light quotient is a measurement of a person's ability to work with and understand spirituality. This concept is compared to the intelligence quotient (IQ). However, in reality, spiritual ability is not related to intelligence, and interestingly, unlike the IQ, one's spiritual light quotient can increase with age and experience.

$16.95 • 384 PP. • Softcover • 978-1-891824-89-0

Connecting with the Arcturians

Who is really out there? Where are we going? What are our choices? What has to be done to prepare for this event? This book explains all of these questions in a way that we can easily understand. It explains what our relationships are to known extraterrestrial groups and what they are doing to help Earth and her people in this crucial galactic moment in time.

$17.00 • 256 PP. • Softcover • 978-1-891824-94-4

New Spiritual Technology for the Fifth-Dimensional Earth

Earth is moving closer to the fifth dimension. New spiritual ideas and technologies are becoming available for rebalancing our world, including native ceremonies to connect to Earth healing energies and thought projections and thought communication with Earth.

$19.95 • 240 PP. • Softcover • 978-1-891824-79-1

♃

⚜ *Light Technology* PUBLISHING *Presents*

THROUGH DAVID K. MILLER

Fifth-Dimensional Soul Psychology

"The basic essence of soul psychology rests with the idea that the soul is evolving and that part of this evolution is occurring through incarnations in the third dimension. Now, to even speak about the soul evolving is perhaps a controversial subject because we know that the soul is eternal. We know that the soul has been in existence for infinity, and we know that the soul is perfect. So why would the soul have to evolve?

The answer to this question is complex, and we may not be able to totally answer it using third-dimensional terminology. But it is an important question to answer, because the nature of soul evolution is inherently connected to your experiences in the third dimension. The soul, in completing its evolutionary journey, needs these experiences in the third dimension, and it needs to complete the lessons here."

—Vywamus

$16.95 • 288 PP. • Softcover • 978-1-62233-016-4

Teachings from the Sacred Triangle, Vol. 1

David's second book explains how the Arcturian energy melds with that of the White Brother-/Sisterhood and the ascended Native American masters to bring about planetary healing.

Topics include the Sacred Triangle energy and the sacred codes of ascension, how to create a bridge to the fifth dimension, what role you can play in the Sacred Triangle, and how sacred words from the Kaballah can assist you in your ascension work.

$16.95 • 288 PP. • Softcover • 978-1-62233-007-2

Teachings from the Sacred Triangle, Vol. 2

Our planet is at a dire crossroads from a physical standpoint, but from a spiritual standpoint, it is experiencing a great awakening. Never before have there been so many conscious lightworkers, awakened spiritual beings, and masters as there are on this planet now. A great sense of a spiritual harmony emanates from the many starseed groups, and there is also a new spiritual energy and force that is spreading throughout the planet.

$16.95 • 288 PP. • Softcover • 978-1-891824-19-7

Teachings from the Sacred Triangle, Vol. 3

Learn how to use holographic technology to project energies in the most direct and transformative way throughout Earth.

Chapters Include:
• Heart Chakra and the Energy of Love
• Multidimensional Crystal Healing Energy
• Healing Space-Time Rifts
• Integration of Spirituality and Technology, Space, and Time Travel

$16.95 • 288 PP. • Softcover • 978-1-891824-23-4

Enseñanzas del Sagrado Triángulo Arcturiano

Este paradigma es necesario para ayudar en la transición de la humanidad hacia la próxima etapa evolutiva. La humanidad debe realizar esta próxima etapa de la evolución, para asegurar su sobrevivencia por los cambios climáticos globales, la guerra y la destrucción del medio ambiente. ¿Cuál es la próxima etapa? Esta involucra la expansión de la consciencia del ser humano y está representada por el símbolo de este nuevo paradigma, el Sagrado Triángulo Arcturiano.

El guía de la quinta dimensión, Juliano, proveniente del sistema estelar galáctico conocido como Arcturus, trabaja junto a David en un papel prominente en esta introducción de la energía del Triángulo Sagrado en la Tierra. David le ofrece al lector un entendimiento del alma, su naturaleza evolutiva y como la humanidad esta avanzando hacia esa siguiente etapa evolutiva.

$19.95 • 416 PP. • Softcover • 978-1-62233-264-9

Expand Your Consciousness

Now more than ever, humankind is in need of developing its higher consciousness to heal itself and Earth and to experience life in a much more meaningful way. By expanding our consciousness, we can see the connections and unity that exist in all reality, and we might see objects with sharper colors, hear sounds with greater clarity, or even experience two sensations simultaneously! In this book, you will explore the fascinating multidimensionality that is yours for the taking.

$16.95 • 288 PP. • Softcover • 978-1-62233-036-2

THROUGH ROBERT SHAPIRO

TOTALITY AND BEYOND

The Search for the Origin of Life — and Beyond

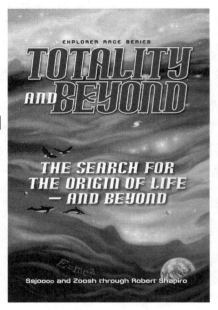

The book you are about to read attempts to explain and, to a degree, put an order to existence. You might reasonably ask, "What is the purpose?" The purpose is very simply this: In order for you now to be able to function in a world of responsibilities well beyond your own physical life, you need to be able to understand the functionality of creation and the confidence you need to have in simply emerging from seemingly nothing. "Nothing" is not really zero. Nothing is a matrix available to create something. It will always be that, and it has always been that. This book will explain, with some wide variety of points of view at times, those points, and over the next few hundred years, you can consider them as you blend with your total being, creating and re-creating what is now, in order to bring it to a more benevolent state of being.

—Ssjoooo, September 18, 2015

$24.95 • Softcover • 416 PP.
978-1-891824-75-3

CHAPTERS INCLUDE:
- The Thirteen Envision the Worlds Within Worlds
- The Loop of Time
- An Unending Parade of Existence
- Disentanglement
- Disentangling Cords of Discomfort
- All Creation Responds to Need
- Every Action Has a Reaction: It's Mother Nature's Plan
- Love and Care for Others to Embrace the Totality
- Feel Heat to Learn Oneness
- You Planned Your Journey
- The Reservoir of Being
- Take Your Journey
- You Must Qualify for Physicality
- Beyond